Black Girl Auto-poetics

Black

Duke University Press   *Durham and London*   2024

Girl Auto-poetics

Agency in Everyday Digital Practice

Ashleigh Greene Wade

WITH ILLUSTRATIONS
BY AL VALENTÍN

© 2024 Duke University Press
All rights reserved
Printed in the United States of America on acid-free paper ∞
Designed by Courtney Leigh Richardson
Typeset in Portrait and IBM Plex Sans by Copperline Book Services

Library of Congress Cataloging-in-Publication Data
Names: Wade, Ashleigh Greene, [date] author. | valentin, al
Title: Black girl autopoetics : agency in everyday digital practice /
Ashleigh Greene Wade ; with illustrations by Al Valentín.
Description: Durham : Duke University Press, 2024. | Includes bibliographical
references and index.
Identifiers: LCCN 2023025642 (print)
LCCN 2023025643 (ebook)
ISBN 9781478025603 (paperback)
ISBN 9781478020851 (hardcover)
ISBN 9781478027737 (ebook)
Subjects: LCSH: Internet and women—United States. | African American women—
Social aspects. | Women—Identity. | Digital media—Social aspects—United States. |
Technology and women—United States. | Technology and Black people—United
States. | African American women in popular culture—History—21st century. |
BISAC: SOCIAL SCIENCE / Ethnic Studies / American / African American & Black Studies |
SOCIAL SCIENCE / Media Studies
Classification: LCC HQ1178 .W334 2024 (print) | LCC HQ1178 (ebook) |
DDC 004.67/8082—dc23/eng/20230712
LC record available at https://lccn.loc.gov/2023025642
LC ebook record available at https://lccn.loc.gov/2023025643

Cover art: Illustration by Kiyah McBride. Courtesy of the artist.

Publication of this book is supported by Duke University Press's
Scholars of Color First Book Fund.

In memory of my grandmother
Willie Jean Greene,

with whom I shared a love
for words and stories.

Contents

Acknowledgments ix

Introduction: Defining Black Girl Autopoetics 1

Interlude: On Developing Digital Ethics for/with Black Girls 19

1. Places to Be: Black Girls Mapping, Navigating, and Creating Space through Digital Practice 29

2. "You Gotta Show Your Life": Reading the Digital Archives of Everyday Black Girlhood 61

3. "I Love Posting Pictures of Myself!": Hypervisibility as a Politics of Refusal 84

4. Making Time: Black Girls' Digital Activism as Temporal Reclamation 105

Conclusion: What Does Black Girl Autopoetics Make Possible? 127

Notes 133   Bibliography 147   Index 157

Acknowledgments

Writing this book has been an act of love, and I am so grateful to all the people who have helped it come to fruition. Brittney Cooper, I don't have words to capture my gratitude for how you have mentored and cared for me over nearly the last decade. I avoided imposter syndrome in graduate school because you always gassed me up and made me feel like I could accomplish any and everything. I appreciate you always.

I want to thank Nikol Alexander-Floyd, Jack Bratich, and Judith Gerson. Your genuine belief in the value of my research and support of my career have been invaluable in shaping me as a scholar and writer. Nicole Fleetwood, thank you for pushing me to theorize in my writing.

Research for this book was supported by a predoctoral fellowship at the University of Virginia's Carter G. Woodson Institute. I am grateful for the conviviality of my cohort and the guidance of faculty during my time there. I especially want to thank Meredith Clark and Cori Field for offering constructive feedback on my work.

I could not have made it to this point without the mentorship of Black women scholars. Ruth Nicole Brown, thank you for being a champion of my work and for years of ongoing support. Gabrielle Foreman, you inspire me, and I appreciate how you've always looked out for me, even before we became colleagues at Penn State. Shirley Moody-Turner, thank you for your insight on my manuscript, helping me navigate my first years on the tenure track, and seeing leadership potential in me. It was a joy to codirect the Cooper-Du Bois Mentoring Program with you. Jessica M. Johnson, I appreciate your invitations into spaces and conversations that have elevated my thinking and my career. Kinitra Brooks, thanks for sincere advice and encouragement.

I drafted this book during my time at Pennsylvania State University, and the Mellon Just Transformations Fellowship sponsored by the Center for Black Digital Research made completion possible. Thank you to my CBDR colleagues for both informal and formal commentary on my work in progress. I also benefitted from the English Department's book manuscript workshop program. Catherine Squires, I appreciate you serving as an external reader for this workshop. Your thorough, encouraging critique helped me polish the final manuscript. I also appreciate Matt Tierney, Christian Haynes, and Tina Chen for their careful attention to the book's development.

I have relied on writing accountability partners to help me move this project forward, especially AnneMarie Mingo, through Sister Scholars, and Dehanza Rogers. Also, thank you Betsy Fauntleroy for allowing me to use your home to hold a personal writing retreat that propelled me to the finish line.

Along with professional relationships and mentorship, life-giving friendships have been essential to the completion of this project. Aria Halliday, my sister, your words of wisdom over the years have sustained me. Thanks for being a constant rider, coconspirator, and friend. Timeka Tounsel, what started out as a collegial collaboration has become one of my most valued friendships. Thank you for reading this entire manuscript and building my confidence as a writer. To my Rutgers fam: Al Valentín, Lexi Smith, Rosemary Ndubizu, and Marlene Gaynair, thanks for your camaraderie during and beyond doctoral studies.

This book would not exist without the community and participation of dozens of Black girls in Richmond, Virginia, and throughout the country. To the Black girls I've taught (and who have taught me), the Black girls who've shared their time with me, the Black girls who allowed me into their spaces to tell me about their lives: thank you. I pray you see yourselves in these pages and in worlds worthy of your brilliance.

To my family: I am appreciative of how you believe in me and remind me of the importance of balance. My sister-cousins Katherine and Sandra, thanks for celebrating my wins with me. D'Ana, thank you for unconditional companionship.

Ma, thanks for raising me to be the woman I am today. Your pride in me, not only as a scholar but as a human, surpasses any professional achievement or reward.

Tyrone, my favorite person, thank you for dreaming with me. The best part of my life is sharing it with you.

PART OF CHAPTER 4 draws from a previous article entitled "Radical Curation: Making Space for Black Childhood(s) in the Art Hoe Collective," which appears in *Visual Arts Research* 47, no. 1 (Summer 2021): 13–28.

Introduction

Defining Black Girl Autopoetics

November 24, 2016: I was back home in Kinston, North Carolina, visiting family for Thanksgiving at my maternal grandparents' house, the house that has been the center of our family functions since it was built in the 1950s. This Thanksgiving, it was unseasonably warm—even for Kinston—but the warmth was not the only unusual thing about that day. This particular Thanksgiving was the first one any of us had celebrated without our family matriarch, my grandmother, who died unexpectedly a couple of months before. So, the mood was heavy as we were still navigating the newness of her absence.

As the day progressed, we eased into our normal traditions: the prayer, the meal, the conversations, the laughter. As much of a staple as the turkey, post-dinner activities involved the grown folks sitting in the kitchen talking while the children—five girls ranging in age from six to twelve—played outside. After being outside almost all afternoon, the girls came in the house excited to show us what they had been doing all day: making a video on Triller.[1] The song they chose as the backdrop of their production came from the viral "You Name It" meme, which featured an excerpt from Shirley Caesar's "Hold My Mule" set to a hip-hop beat by DJ Suede the Remix God. Each girl had a part, and the oldest one edited the video to make the choreography flow seamlessly with the lyrics of the song in the background. Aside from thinking the finished product was incredibly cute, the video intensified my growing interest in the mundane nature of digital technologies in the lives of children living in the United States and how the ubiquitous nature of these technologies shapes what it means to be a Black girl in this moment, a moment in which they do not have to wait for magazines, television networks, and film production companies to produce the media they want to see. In fact, Black girls have the tools at their disposal to produce *their own media*—creating media as play, as communication, as an outlet. This book is about Black girls' everyday digital practices, what their digital content reveals about their everyday experiences, and how their digital productions contribute to a broader record of Black life. In what follows, I weave together a series of stories of how Black girls create spaces and discourse through their digital media production. I do not present the digital (or Black girls' digital content) as a clear-cut example of or avenue toward Black liberation. Instead, I present these stories as a provocation to (re)evaluate processes that are integral to Black life—space-making, archiving, communicating, and organizing—through the lens of Black girlhood. Black girls' digital practices constitute a means through which they invent and reinvent themselves, in turn, inventing and reinventing what it means to live, create, and preserve Black life.

The Stakes: The Social Backdrop of Black Girls' Digital Practices

To understand the creative and disruptive power of Black girls' digital practices requires an examination of the sociopolitical contexts in which their digital content emerges. The digital landscape is neither the utopia early proponents thought or hoped it would be nor the utterly depraved hellscape technophobes cautioned us against. Instead, like every other space occupied by humans, the digital is fraught with ambivalence, which this text cannot escape in its focus on Black girls. While I center Black girls' creativity, I cannot discuss that creativity without acknowledging the clear and present danger of the internet for Black girls.

While the social backdrop of Black girls' digital practices could make up an entire monograph by itself, a life-changing moment for seventeen-year-old Darnella Frazier captures the multifaceted, multilayered "matrix of domination" that shapes Black girls' experiences in the United States.[2] In Minneapolis, Minnesota, on May 25, 2020, Frazier walked her nine-year-old cousin Judeah Reynolds to a local corner store to get some candy. What should have been an uneventful occurrence in the lives of two Black girls turned into a nightmare as the street right in front of the store became the scene of yet another police murder of a Black person: George Floyd. Frazier recorded the murder on her cell phone and posted it to social media that night as a way of witnessing the tragedy and seeking justice.[3] Frazier's impulse to record and share Floyd's murder reflects an instinct that has developed as a result of the quotidian nature of police violence against Black civilians.[4] Inextricably linked to the all-too-familiar violation of Black people at the hands of police, fear of incredibility drives the need to record police murders. Ironically, the fact that few police officers have been charged with or convicted of crimes, even with video evidence, bolsters the impulse to record police violence because Black people feel (read: know) that if investigators will not believe the video evidence before their eyes, they certainly will not believe the testimony of a Black person. For Frazier, her age, race, and gender all shape perceptions about her believability within a white supremacist heteropatriarchy. Given these realities, Frazier's act of recording was, unfortunately, not abnormal or exceptional.

Recalling the incident, Frazier explained, "They killed this man. And I was right there! I was like five feet away! It is so traumatizing."[5] Now This, an online, video-based news-media company, reported about Frazier, but not everyone saw her as a hero. Some people began to bully Frazier online, claiming that she posted the video for attention and suggesting that she should have physically intervened instead of recording the murder on her cell phone.[6] Since the bullying, Frazier has not spoken to media sources, but she did post on her Facebook page:

> I'm doing it for clout?? For attention?? What?? To get paid?? Now y'all just sound dumb and ignorant!! I don't expect anyone who wasn't placed in my position to understand why and how I feel the way that I do!! MIND YOU I am a minor! 17 years old, of course I'm not about to fight off a cop I'm SCARED wtf. If it wasn't for me 4 cops would've still had their jobs, causing other problems. My video went world wide for everyone to see and know!! His family was reached out to! The police most definitely would've swept it under the rug with a cover up story. Instead of bashing me, THANK ME! Because that could've been one of your loved ones and you would want to see the truth as well.[7]

Frazier's response to these bullies reflects both the level of vitriol spewed at her and her psychological and emotional trauma.

The attacks on Frazier put a spotlight on the threats Black girls face online. In some ways, the structure of social media sites makes cyberbullying and harassment easy to enact without consequences. While Facebook requires users to provide their given names on their profiles, other sites like Instagram, You-

Tube, Snapchat, and Twitter allow users to choose a screen name that is not necessarily the same or related to names on their official identification documents, thereby fostering a sense of anonymity that emboldens potential bullies.[8] Additionally, people create fake accounts. Sometimes these accounts are bots, a form of artificial intelligence (AI), and other times hackers and trolls create fake accounts posing as a real person—a form of digital identity theft. While these features of social media already create ripe conditions for cyberbullying, algorithms have the potential to intensify online harassment. Major tech companies use algorithms to increase their profit margins, oftentimes at the expense of marginalized folks.[9] While there have been recent campaigns to put pressure on companies like Twitter and Facebook to do more extensive content monitoring, the same algorithms that can make a cat meme go viral can also make disparaging comments about Black girls go viral. In Frazier's case, the viral video that she shared made her more exposed, and therefore a more susceptible target for bullying. Despite popular social media applications having policies about online harassment, algorithms tend to feed the trolls because more reacting, commenting, and sharing—regardless of the nature of the content—means more revenue for these companies.

Cyberbullying—and the algorithms that fuel it—does not pose a unique threat to Black girls, but the backlash leveled against Frazier illustrates how online harassment can be driven and exacerbated by misogynoir.[10] The expectation that Frazier, a child, would approach four armed adults—already in the process of killing another adult—to stop them exemplifies many people's inability to see Black girls as innocent, to see them as deserving of joy and peace, and to see them as children. Based on the evidence that points to how Black girls in the United States are seen as adults earlier than their white counterparts, it would be hard to believe a white girl who witnessed a murder before her very eyes would have been met with judgment and bullying for not intervening. Most likely a white girl in Frazier's position would have been called a hero for filming the incident and people would have questioned the moral fiber of a group of police officers who could do such a thing in front of a perceivably innocent little girl.[11] Another way that the attacks on Frazier illustrate misogynoir lies in how the video garnered sympathy for George Floyd (as it should have) and galvanized protests around the world in his honor while Frazier's trauma, along with Black girls' collective trauma in general, dropped from our purview. To be clear, I am not juxtaposing Floyd and Frazier to engage in a form of oppression Olympics that would measure compassion and sympathy based on identity categories or personal traits. Instead, I am pointing out how the story of Frazier—a Black girl—dropped from the conversation about how (police) violence impacts Black families and communities, further illustrating how the violation and endangerment of Black girls and women does not generate the same collective sense of urgency as that of Black boys and men.

Darnella Frazier's story is a high-profile case that helps to consolidate key features of the social climate in which Black girls have to be creative. Unfortunately, Frazier's situation brings renewed attention to an old problem: the paradox of Black girls' hyper(in)visibility. On the one hand, Black girls' online activity makes them hypervisible and, in turn, creates a "scopic vulnerability" that puts them at risk for cyberbullying, harassment, and other forms of violence.[12] On the other hand, Black girls get lost in digital contexts on (at least) two levels. One, we lose the voices, stories, and identities of Black girls in how people respond to them in contexts of hypervisibility. For instance, when people use Black girls' digital content to make reductive generalizations, Black girls' voices are often absent from the discourse that arises. Two, after the moment of hypervisibility passes, Black girls' stories get lost among continuously updating newsfeeds and talking heads pontificating. In Frazier's case, even as news stories continued to talk about George Floyd, the girl behind the video got buried further. This act of moving on has not transpired out of respect for Frazier's privacy; instead, it is on par with how noise of seemingly more important issues drowns out Black girls' stories.

Along with violence, the paradox of hyper(in)visibility makes Black girls more susceptible to (hyper)sexualization and criminalization, and amateur video platforms have played a central role in depicting Black girls as overly sexual criminals. As Safiya Noble points out, these platforms facilitate and perpetuate a form of algorithmic violence that increases the likelihood for these types of dehumanizing images to appear in online searches for Black girls.[13] For example, entertainment site World Star Hip Hop helped popularize the video genre featuring Black girls fighting. The 2013 viral video of Sharkeisha Thompson attacking ShaMichael Manuel made its way from Vine to World Star and received millions of views. Instead of generating a sense of concern about the conditions—psychological or otherwise—that catalyzed the fight, the video, and the girls it depicted, became the butt of jokes and evidence of Black girls' presumed propensity for violence and criminality. Although the Sharkeisha video did not have an explicitly sexual nature, videos of Black girls fighting and Black girls twerking go hand in hand when it comes to Black girls' hyper(in)visibility. Twerking is a dance style that involves gyration and rapid movement of the butt, which makes many people perceive it as inherently sexual. Therefore, people invested in Black girls' denigration point to videos of them twerking online as confirmation of their supposed sexual proclivity. These discursive discrepancies between how Black girls dance and how other people perceive them sometimes translates to material harm. As ethnomusicologist and Black girlhood studies pioneer Kyra Gaunt argues, Black girls' twerking videos on YouTube can make them victims of "digital sexploitation."[14] Gaunt's research uncovers how "Black girls are doubly-exploited" by adults (especially men) and YouTube as a corporation when they post twerking videos on the platform.[15] YouTube makes money off Black girls' twerking videos through Google AdSense, and the songs that form the soundtracks of these videos generate profit for (mostly) male artists.[16] On a more violent level, grown men have subjected young Black (and Brown) girls to predatory, sexually explicit comments as well as doxxing. Historically, YouTube has done little to nothing to stop, investigate, or remove predatory, pornographic comments grown men make on young Black girls' twerking videos. To be clear, Black girls have no responsibility to debunk stereotypes about their sexualities, nor should they be denied opportunities to find embodied pleasure. Therefore, I do not mention twerking videos here to suggest Black girls modify their online presentation, though they may want to mitigate these potential harms by doing so. Instead, I point to people's reductive interpretations of Black girls twerking as an example of how hyper(in)visibility maps onto Black girls' digital content. While there are seemingly countless examples of the dangers facing Black girls, the aforementioned instances of harassment, criminalization, and (hyper)sexualization epitomize the social backdrop against which Black girls engage the digital because they reflect a convergence of forces working against them (both on and offline), robbing them of their innocence and joy. The dangers that I have outlined here can stifle Black girls' creativity. So, Black girls' continued creation and re-creation—through media, stories, and art—in the face of danger represents a power struggle where Black girls work to shift power away from the forces that seek to destroy them. This creative process helps Black girls assert themselves within and against systems so quick to exploit and discard them.

The Sites: Locating and Collaborating with Black Girls

For the purposes of this research, I defined *Black girlhood* using the following parameters. Even though the research focuses on girls based in the United States, I use the word *Black* or *Black American* instead of *African American* to reflect the ethnic diversity of US-based Black people. To define *girl*, I used gender expression and the legal age of adulthood in the United States as primary indicators. However, since the legal age of adulthood is arbitrary, I also used experience as an additional marker.[17] While the book aims to extend our conceptions of

Black girls' subjectivities beyond their roles as students, I still use participation in (or being of an age to participate in) primary and secondary school as an experience that defines girlhood since K–12 school attendance or affiliation tends to be a marker of childhood in the United States.

Given the paradox of hyper(in)visibility, an examination of Black girls' digital practices must not only locate Black girls but must also find where and how Black girls tell their own stories. In committing to the journey of learning more about what Black girls do online, I knew I would have to peruse digital spaces. However, my reading of Black girls' digital content, while rooted in established analytical methodologies, is informed by my own acquired, embodied, and lived knowledge.[18] Therefore, telling the story of Black girls' digital practices required going directly to the source.

Driven by the impetus to center Black girls' voices, I decided to combine my own interpretation of their content with ethnography. In the spirit of scholars like Moya Bailey and LeConté Dill, who viewed research participants as collaborators and coresearchers, respectively, I engaged Black girl interlocutors both in person and online.[19] For the physical site research, I conducted participant-observation, interviews, and discussion groups with Black girls in Richmond, Virginia.[20] I chose Richmond as a site for understanding everyday Black girlhood for several reasons. Richmond has been and remains a prominent location for Black cultural production, as evidenced by the inclusion of Black Richmonders in the historical accounts of the city's museums and other cultural institutions. Given Richmond's historical relevance and contemporary developments, Richmond has emerged as a Southern, urban arts hub in its own right. For instance, the largest university in the city, Virginia Commonwealth University, hosts a nationally ranked visual arts program, and the Virginia Museum of Fine Arts features a number of world-renowned exhibitions that have included Deborah Willis's *Posing Beauty* (2013) and Kehinde Wiley's *New Republic* (2016). Richmond's burgeoning reputation as an art city was significant to this project because it meant there were a number of youth-serving organizations in the area that expose children to artistic techniques, including photography and film. Even though the research focuses on more mundane media production (as opposed to media produced within formal institutional contexts), these art organizations proved to be a productive starting point for finding Black girls to talk to about their digital content.

Another reason I chose Richmond has to do with situating the United States South more prominently within conversations about youth and digital technologies. The representative studies on youth and digital media in the United States do not focus much on youth in the South even though, according to census data, the majority of Black Americans still live in the South; Atlanta, Georgia, is the exception.[21] Richmond is one of many cities in the South where Black people make up the largest percent of the population. This statistical reality along with Richmond's role in Black culture helped solidify the city's relevance to a study about everyday Blackness.

Richmond's significant Black population in combination with its historical and contemporary importance to Black cultural production played a role in my decision to conduct research there, but I also had personal ties to the city. I moved to Richmond in 2008 to pursue a master's degree at the University of Richmond, and after finishing the degree program, I began teaching English and history at an independent (private) all-girls school in the area in 2010, the same year that Snapchat launched. I elaborate more on the confluence of conditions that drove me to want to learn more about Black girls' digital spaces in chapter 1, but my observations of how the Black girls who frequented my classroom used Snapchat (and social media in general) made me keenly aware of commonalities in Black girls' experiences of restriction, particularly in school settings, even when they had access to the resources that people claimed would be a panacea to all the problems in public schools. In this way, choosing Richmond as a research site was also about going back to the place that set me on the path to learn more about Black girls' digital practices in order to make sense of their experiences within broader sociocultural contexts.

I found Richmond to be an important, relevant site to study Black girls' digital practices, and I learned a great deal from the girls who shared their time, thoughts, and stories with me. However, I knew I wanted to engage with Black girls throughout the country to get deeper immersion into their everyday lives at the intersection of the digital. To find more Black girls to engage with online, I turned to the census. The United States Census Bureau released "The Black Population: 2010," a report that offers in-depth discussion of Black American demographic data.[22] The report includes two top-ten lists: one of the ten cities with the highest number of Black people and another of the ten cities that had the largest percentage of Black people. Using these lists, I looked up predominantly Black high schools in these nineteen cities.[23] Then I looked for Instagram profiles that had geotagged these high schools in their posts. Not all of the people posting about these high schools were students or children, so I only examined profiles of Black girls who indicated they were students at the schools—usually they would include something like "South High School, class of . . ." or "student at South High School." I also used posts about participation in school-sanctioned, extracurricular activities to determine school affiliation.

Once I located the profiles of several Black girls using this method, I would check to see who commented on their posts to find additional hundreds of Black girls. I used Instagram and these specific cities as a starting point for searching for Black girls online, but many of them would often have information about their other social media accounts (Snapchat and YouTube mostly) on their Instagram profiles, so I used that information to find more Black girls across platforms and in several locations. As much as possible, I checked people's profiles for information that would give me clues that they identified as Black and a girl, but in some instances, I did rely on a combination of phenotypical features and cultural signifiers to determine race and gender.

Methodologically, finding Black girls involves more than locating them. While I used the tools and resources above to search for and locate Black girls, *finding* them means learning (from and with) them. Ethically, this process of finding Black girls translates to asserting their right to be heard and understood in addition to being seen. Through this process of finding, we come to see Black life through the lens of Black girlhood, which adds nuance to critiques of broad social structures and sheds light on both inter- and intragroup dynamics that go unnoticed when we do not learn (from) Black girls. Therefore, Black girls' perspectives play an essential role in chronicling, analyzing, and understanding Black life.

The Invention: Black Girl Autopoetics

I would eventually come to understand what my cousins created—along with the digital content of hundreds of other Black girls—as a product of Black girl autopoetics. To think through autopoetics as a concept and a practice, I draw from Sylvia Wynter's theorizations and analyses of poesis and autopoiesis from the 1970s into the twenty-first century. In a 1976 conference talk entitled "Ethno or Socio Poetics," Wynter uses George Quasha's definition of ethnopoetics, breaking the term down to its roots, in order to convey a broad application of "poetics." Quoting Quasha, Wynter defines poesis as "acts of 'making.'"[24] Building on this definition, Wynter goes on to explain poetry—the outcome of poesis—as an instrument for "naming" and "conceptualizing" that allows for the "invention and reinvention of humanness" as well as the reinterpretation/repurposing of semiotic meaning.[25] Further expanding her definition of poetics in an interview with Greg Thomas of *ProudFlesh*, Wynter clarified that she doesn't discuss "poetics or poesis . . . as some narrow, literary affair" but instead attributes poetics to the "continuation of humanness" through its deliberate and ongoing rejection of Man (which Wynter defines as white, Judeo-Christian, bourgeoisie, cisgender, heterosexual male) as the generic human in exchange for more livable, infinitely heterogenous ways of being.[26] For Wynter, poetics reflects a nonlinear mode of thinking, theorizing, and creating.

These musings help illustrate the functions and power of poetics, but according to Wynter, people are not naturally or instinctively inclined to question the social systems that valorize Man as the generic, right way to be human. Instead, the inventive, counter-hegemonic potentialities of poetics must be awakened. In an interview with Katherine McKittrick, Wynter delves into the concept of autopoiesis using Maturana and Varela's *Autopoiesis and Cognition* as a point of reference and departure. Maturana and Varela describe autopoiesis as a self-replicating function and use the term in a strict biological context. However, Wynter applies this concept to human social structures, noting our tendency to replicate the status quo, oftentimes without even realizing we are doing so. She uses bees in a hive as an analogy to describe how autopoiesis applies to human societies: "So that in the same way as the bee can never have knowledge of the higher-level system that is its hive, we too can in no way normally gain cognitive access to the higher level of the genre-specific autopoietic living system of our status quo structured social worlds."[27] In other words, the repetition of and complicity in the status quo obscure our agential capacities to create ourselves and live our lives differently. Though Wynter identifies autopoiesis as a process of reproduction and replication, she does not concede this process as one beyond breach. As McKittrick points out, Wynter's concept of autopoiesis is about breaching the "recursive logic" that "depicts our presently ecocidal and genocidal world as normal and unalterable."[28] Using Fanon's "out-of-body" third-person consciousness and Du Bois's double-consciousness, Wynter describes how people become aware of their existence in relation to Man.[29] That moment of recognition "provide[s] the conditions to assert different living systems and/or breach the existing social system" through "creative human aesthetics that generate a point of view *away* from this consensual circular system."[30] It is from this rupture that I theorize Black girl autopoetics.

I define Black girl autopoetics (BGA) as an inherently spatiotemporal praxis of creation. In breaking down autopoiesis to its roots, the word translates to self-making. I deploy the concept of self-making in two ways: Black girls making themselves (i.e., their subjectivities) and Black girls staking claim to a creative process that is their own (i.e., making *for* themselves). I present BGA as a praxis of creation because it encompasses how Black girls (re)invent cultural products, spaces, and discourses in their subjective formation and expression. Throughout this text, when I refer to Black girls' creativity I do not mean this as a conflation with artistry—even though art is part of Black girls' creative repertoire. Instead, I am using creativity to mean inclined toward creation. Black people have created (and continue to create) alternate, new worlds within the worlds we were not meant to survive.[31] Therefore, BGA functions as a world-making technology; it is both theory of the flesh and a survival methodology rooted in Black girls' ways of knowing and making meaning. BGA aligns with Aisha Durham's conception of "life affirming poetics," which "emerge from a doing, knowing body whose historical, conjunctural speech-bodily-written acts are sometimes irreconcilable and deliberate but never detached."[32] These embodied, affective epistemologies simultaneously reflect Black girls' individual lived experiences and collective, intra- and intergenerational exchanges.

My theorization of BGA is not meant to be a proscriptive—meaning there is no litmus test for measuring if something is or isn't Black girl autopoetics. Instead, BGA is characterized by the ways that Black girls make a way out of no way and carve new paths on old roads. BGA includes Black girls creating spaces for themselves within institutions that try to shut them out, Black girls dancing through the streets of Detroit, Black girls writing poetry and making music with each other.[33] Therefore, Black girls' digital content is not the only source of BGA. However, BGA makes Black girls' digital media production unique: other girls may engage similar processes of self-making in digital spaces, but BGA cannot be separated from the lived experiences and consequences of being a Black girl in worlds built on and sustained by white supremacy and misogynoir: "Being a blackgirl means something specific and carries with it the meanings and microaggressions blackgirls live with everyday."[34] This book demonstrates how Black girls' digital media production elucidates the salient features of BGA in hopes of offering an approach to chronicling and interpreting Black experiences in ways that seek out and pay attention to the often overlooked, unheard voices and stories that are no less valuable to understanding and preserving Black life than the ones that tend to occupy more space in our collective Black imaginaries.

Black Girl Autopoetics as Theory

One of the key interventions of the rapidly expanding field of Black girlhood studies is that not only does it approach Black girls from a point of productivity rather than deficiency, but it also centers Black girls as cultural producers and theorists. While Black girlhood studies itself has grown from the premise that Black girls' stories are inherently valuable to knowledge-production, other fields of study conversant with this work—Black studies, visual or media studies—have not always been intentional about including the voices of children or adolescents. Therefore, cultural studies fields as a whole still need more accounts of Black girls' experiences in their own words, and these accounts should represent the range of subjective complexities that Black girls embody. Given the prevalence of digital technologies, contending with their role in Black girls' everyday lives and practices not only contributes to a greater understanding of Black girls' lived experiences and realities but also allows for a deeper understanding of Black girls as cultural producers. Taking this radical approach to children's cultural production, Black girlhood studies demonstrates how Black girls (and children in general) are relevant to cultural theory and praxis.

As Black girlhood studies continues to evolve as a field, the question of theoretical frameworks—both informing and emerging from Black girlhood studies—becomes more pressing.[35] While the relationship between Black girlhood studies and Black feminism may seem obvious, there are tensions that exist regarding recognizing Black girlhood as a distinct stage from Black womanhood and, in turn, a distinct source of cultural theory. Black feminism clearly informs many of the displays of Black girlhood that I discuss throughout this text. At the same time, as a framework generally formed from the experiences of *adult* Black women, Black feminism can sometimes obscure the *girl*-specific elements of Black girls' lived knowledges. #BlackGirlMagic helps elucidate this elision. In their foundational collection, Julia Jordan-Zachery and Duchess Harris present #BlackGirlMagic as "one manifestation of Black women's political and cultural behaviors."[36] Despite the word *girl*, #BlackGirlMagic "is not bound by chronological age or society's conceptualization of moving into adulthood."[37] This fluidity allows the girl within #BlackGirlMagic to operate as an intragroup, "community-building" tool across age, which then facilitates crucial elements of Black feminist politics such as reclamation, restoration, and self-definition.[38] At the same time, #BlackGirlMagic's all-age inclusivity eclipses Black girls' distinct experiential epistemologies. In fact, when I brought up #BlackGirlMagic in discussions with Black girls while conducting research, none of them identified with the concept, which speaks to how Black women's feminist frameworks do not automatically align with the experiences of Black girls.[39] I do not mean to suggest that Black women simply throw away their childhoods when constructing Black feminist theory. Instead, I am pointing out a difference between theorizing through *reflection upon* girlhood and theorizing from *within the stage* of girlhood.

Black girlhood studies pioneer Ruth Nicole Brown has been calling attention to the unique and specific qualities of theorizing Black girls' lives. Brown makes important distinctions between Black girlhood studies theory and Black feminist theory, noting that while Black girls may "speak and enact Black womanist/

feminist sensibilities and actions," Black girls have their own epistemologies that stem from what they know *themselves*, not from what adults claim to know about them.[40] That is not to say that Black girls cannot be Black feminists or that they cannot use Black feminist (or womanist) theory, but Black girlhood has its own frameworks.[41] These frameworks may be derived from and/or adjacent to Black feminism but not always necessarily captured by Black feminist theories rooted in the experiences of Black women. Therefore, my conceptualization of BGA presents it as both a theory that emerges from the study of Black girlhood and a hermeneutic for apprehending Black girls' socialities, which in this case includes their digital practices.

I want to be careful in outlining these distinctions between BGA and Black feminism as they correspond to differences between Black girls and women and not fall into a trap of essentialism, exclusion, and/or proscription. I recognize that Black feminist theory is applicable to, useful to, and concerned with Black people who do not necessarily identify as women or girls. However, I make these distinctions as a way to be attentive to how Black girls' specific needs, desires, and epistemologies get lost when we do not acknowledge girlhood as a distinct stage.[42]

In addition to illustrating the complex relationship between Black feminist theory and Black girlhood studies, BGA provides nuanced approaches to Black visuality at the intersection of Black girlhood. Visuality as a concept has undergone intense revision as more scholars bring intersectional cultural analyses to visual studies. BGA adds to conversations of Black visuality by suggesting that Black girls' production of visual content within digital spaces unsettles some of the traditional (i.e., predigital era) Black feminist literature regarding visual representation of Black girls' and women's bodies. BGA advances conversations regarding Black visuality by showing how the visual field is not inherently harmful to Black girls and women. Of course, we have to remain vigilant about the circulation and appropriation of Black girls' images, but the creative functions of BGA challenge a facile producer-consumer binary and in turn push past a totalizing characterization of visual media that sees Black girls only as victims of technology rather than innovators within a system designed for their exclusion and optimized for their degradation. BGA shows how even though Black girls are participating in media production largely through corporate-driven applications, they can create and share visual media in ways that are not available to them with television and film. In an age of digital (social) media, Black girls do not have to wait to be reflected in the dominant popular imaginary or "unmirrored" by a lack of (undistorted) representation.[43]

Introduction 13

Black Girl Autopoetics as Praxis

Despite interventions related to issues of online privacy, media-based moral panics, and self-branding, approaches to media and girlhood rarely place emphasis on what girls *produce* with digital technologies.[44] Notable exceptions include Mary Celeste Kearney and Sharon Mazzarella. Kearney published the "first book-length study of contemporary U.S. girls' media production," which highlights and analyzes girl-produced media ranging from music to zines to films.[45] Likewise, Mazzarella's scholarship has centered girls' media-making in broader discourses of youth, digital technologies, and identity development.[46] Building on the work of Kearney and Mazzarella, my approach to Black girls as cultural producers puts Black girlhood studies in conversation with media and technology studies in an effort to understand what looking at the particularities of Black girlhood can tell us broadly about digital media ecologies. While girlhood studies and media studies intersect frequently, scholarship that looks at *Black* girlhood and media is not as robust and/or tends to be focused on consumption.[47] Other studies provide some theorization of Black girls' media production but still indicate consumptive influences as the main indicator of what Black girls will produce in digital spaces.[48] While the aforementioned authors theorize media practices themselves, others have outlined the productive possibilities presented by Black girls' engagements with digital media, conversations this book continues.[49]

As a technology of making, BGA is both theory and praxis, and Black girls' digital practices elucidate the layered textures of Black girls' creativity. I return to my cousins' Triller video to expound upon the various layers of creation within BGA. At the surface, material level the girls created a digital video that they could save, share, and replay. Another level of creation is a spatial one, which makes sense given that Black girlhood is an inherently spatial formation; Black girls' very existence and survival depend on their negotiations of space within and against sociocultural contexts that demand they take up as little space as possible.[50] The theoretical intervention that my work makes into conversations about Black girls' spatialities lies in the exploration of what Black girls' digital media practices reveal about the materiality and spatiality of the digital. Spatially, the video not only occupies bytes within the storage capacities of Triller and the cloud, but it also incorporates how the girls manipulated the physical space of the backyard to stage the video, find props, and create a plot.

The spatial configuration of my cousins' video also leads to a temporal analysis. Even though the girls had no way of knowing they were doing this, they created an intergenerational loop of nostalgia. My first cousins (their moms) and I spent countless days playing in that same backyard as children. Of course, we did not have cell phones to aid in our play. The only props we had were the occasional magnolia leaves that we filled with dirt to create pretend hot dogs for our imaginary restaurant. Don't worry; we didn't actually eat them! Despite the differences between our tech-absent hot dogs and the digitized play represented by their Triller creation, the girls' video transported my first cousins and me back to our childhoods. In creating their own memory of the day, the girls connected their elders to our memories of playing and making as little Black girls.

Along with material and spatiotemporal creations, the girls also created a discourse about the relationship between digital technologies and play. Their video undermines the notion that children playing on their phones automatically stifles creativity and social interactions. In addition to creating the video itself, the girls created a world—however brief or fleeting—where they each had a part to play. In thinking about how the girls played with each other on that day, technology brought their imagined worlds to life. Furthermore, finding an activity that a six-year-old will enjoy as much as a twelve-year-old is not easy. The video, at least in that moment, diminished the significance of age difference in play because they found an activity that held all their interest. For the girls to negotiate those age-difference dynamics in a harmonious way without the supervision of adults demonstrates social skills, which the cell phone facilitated instead of hindered.

To be clear, I am not suggesting that my young cousins consciously created a world-making methodology. As is the case with most everyday cultural products, the intention is more rooted in mundane desires and activities. However, the way I read my cousins' everyday cultural product (and read Black girls' everyday digital practices throughout the text) not only contextualizes the video within its sociocultural moment but also exemplifies BGA and its affective and agential implications.

Chapter Structure

In the chapters that follow, stories and reflections of Black girls' digital practices cohere to illustrate BGA as theory and praxis. Each chapter explores a level of Black girls' creativity—what they create through BGA and what that creation inspires in the (re)evaluation of how we understand integral elements of Black life.

A brief interlude, "On Developing Digital Ethics for/with Black Girls," follows this introduction. The interlude offers a self-reflexive discussion of my methodological choices in designing and conducting the research for this book. Focusing on ethical questions that arose beyond the parameters of the institutional review board (IRB), this section of the text outlines my positionality and considers the complexities of representing Black girls' digital content against an anti-Black, heteropatriarchal gaze.

The first chapter, "Places to Be: Black Girls Mapping, Navigating, and Creating Space through Digital Practice," highlights the function of BGA as a space-making technology. Using ethnographic data from Black girls in Richmond, Virginia, the chapter theorizes Black girls' geographies through the inextricability of their digital content, physical environments, and worldviews. In this chapter, I use Black girls' posts on social media (as well as their commentary about these posts) to construct a theory of the digital as both spatial and material. I argue that Black girls' digital media productions illustrate the interconnected and multilayered spaces that they must navigate, and their movements through these spaces both shape and are shaped by their production of digital content. In addressing the spatiality of the digital, this chapter also explains how Black girls respond to and attempt to control their environments.

Moving from a discussion of how girls make spaces, the second chapter, "'You Gotta Show Your Life': Reading the Digital Archives of Everyday Black Girlhood," demonstrates how the spaces that Black girls have created have allowed informal archives of Black life to materialize. Connecting Black girls' digital image-making to traditions of Black vernacular photography and videography along with the ways Black girls have historically used the media platforms available to them as a means of self-fashioning, I show how Black girls use social media as a means of self-curation—a process that simultaneously involves thoughtful selection of images to share on social media and creates a sense of authority for Black girls regarding their image(s).[51] Some might argue that self-curation encourages or facilitates a false presentation of self, but I argue that Black girls' digital practices in general force us to push back against the tendency to think of digital products as inherently unreal.

Related to these informal archives, the third chapter, "'I Love Posting Pictures of Myself!': Hypervisibility as a Politics of Refusal," shows how Black girls negotiate and play with the (hyper)*visible* aspect of the hyper(in)visibility paradox. Indeed, some Black girls embrace hypervisibility instead of shying away from its potential consequences. Throughout this chapter, I identify three specific, though certainly not exhaustive, genres of hypervisibility in Black girls' online images: ratchet performativity, sexualization, and flexin.[52] I argue that this deliberate act of making oneself hypervisible operates as a form of refusal through which Black girls reject responsibility for an anti-Black image regime that tries to strip them of their expressive agency. Black girls' use of hypervisibility is a tool of BGA, commanding space for disruptive imagery and creating a sense of urgency around taking Black girls' subjective expressions seriously.

Finally, the fourth chapter, "Making Time: Black Girls' Digital Activism as Temporal Reclamation," focuses on Black girls' relationship to time. I take an in-depth look at Black girls and nonbinary teens who use their social media profiles as an integral part of their activist work: Eva Oleita and Ama Russell of Black Lives Matter in All Capacities (BLMIAC), Marley Dias of #1000BlackGirlBooks, and the curators of the Art Hoe Collective. These three activist efforts encapsulate the key tenets of Black time and help expound upon the relationship between BGA, Black girls' digital practices, and time. Adding to the many conversations regarding the political potential of social media, the chapter argues that BGA, as it manifests in Black girls' digital activism, undermines temporal dispossession and equips Black girls with the agency to reclaim, make, and keep time. Ultimately the theorization of Black girls' temporal restructuring positions BGA as a method for creating the conditions for a future that does not yet exist.

The text concludes with a discussion of the possibilities that emerge from looking at Black life through a BGA lens. Even though Black girls' creative practices are specific to their experiences, they have broader implications for how we understand Blackness as it relates to space, memory, representation, and time. Looking at how Black girls deploy BGA in their digital practices offers insight into ways of creating alternative spaces, narratives, and temporalities in the face of white supremacist attempts at Black erasure. The conclusion urges us to listen to Black girls and learn from their techniques of survival.

Interlude

On Developing Digital Ethics for/with Black Girls

One of the most exciting moments in my early academic career happened when I solidified a methodology for studying Black girls' digital practices. As a doctoral student, I had gotten used to describing my proposed project over and over: in every seminar, at conferences, to random strangers who found out I was completing a PhD. Inevitably, in most of these conversations, someone would say: "You're going to have a hard time with the IRB." Hearing that refrain so many times had me shook, but thankfully my experiences working with institutional review boards (IRBs) at several institutions disproved such ominous foreshadowing.[1] Within academia and other nonprofit organizations engaging in human research, the IRB functions as an ethical authority, a safeguard against unethical, exploitative experiments.[2] While the IRB aims to protect all human participants, they have additional guidelines for designated vulnerable populations: pregnant women, fetuses, neonates, children, and prisoners. Among the people who thought I would have trouble securing IRB approval, these additional requirements seemed like a bureaucratic hurdle in the research process. However, the extra protections helped to reinforce my ethical commitments to Black girls.

Ethics should be at the center of all scholarly investigation, whether working in person or online. Digital ethics refers to "the normative principles for action and interaction in digital environments";[3] it encompasses a range of "moral problems related to data, algorithms, and corresponding practices."[4] Such conceptualizations speak broadly to ethical issues at the intersection of the digital, but my Black feminist politics along with my experiences as a former Black girl, a teacher of Black girls, and a scholar of Black girlhood all shape my approach to studying (with) Black girls. Therefore, I wanted to be deliberate about developing an ethical practice of engaging Black girls in digital spaces. Recognizing that Black girls do not owe us access to their interiorities, the digital ethics framework reflected in this book prioritizes a balance between chronicling Black life and protecting Black girls' safe, sacred, private interior spaces. Compliance with the IRB's special considerations for working with children offered an ethical foundation, but looking at digital ethics through a Black girlhood lens necessitates an expansion of institutional ethical standards because of the unique impact misogynoir has on Black girls. Given this reality, I established additional ethical parameters for doing this specific study. These adjustments reflect self-reflexivity, concerns for Black girls' privacy, and considerations of gaze.

Situating Myself within the Research

In drafting my very first IRB protocol, I sat down with a senior professor who had decades of experience with the research approval process. He asked, "How are you going to get girls to talk to you? It's going to take time for them to trust you." His question and the conversation that followed prompted deep consideration of my positionality in this research. Of course, I had studied and discussed ethnographic self-reflexivity in graduate coursework and in preparation for conducting the project. However, up until confronting this question, I had considered self-reflexivity an exercise for outsiders, those doing research about a group to which they did not belong. Despite not being in the stage of girlhood at the commencement of this research, I did not initially see myself as an outsider because, as a child, I navigated many of the same attitudes and (oftentimes deliberate) misunderstandings about Black girlhood as my prospective research participants/collaborators. As a dark-skinned, nappy-haired, precocious Black girl from a poor-to-working-class family, people rarely looked at me and thought I possessed or deserved a sense of childhood innocence.[5] Much like Black girls today, I experienced early adultification and its consequences. Therefore, in my mind, *history* as a former Black girl made me an insider. However, the *present* realities of being a Black woman place me outside of contemporary Black girls' circles because adulthood creates an automatic power differential between my research collaborators and me. Acknowledgment of this power discrepancy required ongoing evaluation of my positionality in both digital and in-person interactions.

After making this preliminary self-reflection, the next opportunity to assess positionality happened during the recruitment process, which involved describing the research and its potential uses to prospective research collaborators and their parents/legal guardians. These informational exchanges outlined the overall purpose of the research: to learn more about Black girls' digital practices and experiences from their own perspectives. Along with making sure to obtain parental consent for girls under eighteen, one ethical consideration in my interactions with individual Black girls involved setting boundaries. Even though all the parents and legal guardians I talked to expressed excitement about their daughters' participation, I ensured parents understood they could not force their daughters to take part in this research. Among girls who agreed to share their experiences, I emphasized their authority to set boundaries around what and how much they wanted to disclose about their digital practices. In practical terms this meant girls could choose whether they wanted to share their social media screen names or profiles and which (if any) of my questions they wanted to answer.[6] In face-to-face conversations with Black girls, I used an audio recorder, and there were times when they would ask me to stop recording so they could talk about more personal matters. This ability to converse off the record offered another way for the girls to set boundaries around what and how much people can know about them. Additionally, these off-the-record conversations tempered some of my power as a researcher because stopping the recording regulated what I could recall and credit to specific girls at specific times. In turn, I had no reliable memory of sensitive discussions that could betray the girls' interior information.

While my interactions with girls in digital spaces certainly required self-reflexivity, the in-person interactions added more layers to addressing ethical questions because there were more people involved in the research process. Online, I communicated with girls directly, but in face-to-face interactions, I had to grapple with the dynamics of specific educational environments in addition to talking to the girls themselves. The discussion groups with Black girls at after-school and summer camp programs required talking to school and program administrators to get permission to speak to the girls and set up times to have our conversations. Those interactions went smoothly in terms of ethical considerations (though there were other issues that arose, which are detailed in chapter 3). However, the field site that presented the most ethical challenges, especially in relation to environment, was Liberty Preparatory School (Liberty

Prep), where I spent one semester doing participant-observation as a volunteer teacher for a proposed elective course entitled Digital Expressions.[7] To start, there was a disconnect between the course's research goals and the school's disciplinary nature; I wanted to learn from Black girls about their digital practices, and the school administrators wanted me to teach them about what they should and should not post online. Without yielding to the administrators' expectations, I designed the curriculum to address issues of media literacy while still prioritizing students' experiences with using digital technologies. Along with these philosophical discrepancies, interpersonal communication presented a challenge as some of the school personnel upheld misogynoir in the ways they treated Black girls. Through constant policing of Black girls' speech, clothing, mannerisms, and so-called bad attitudes, these staff members saw Black girls as problems to be solved—or worse, removed. Therefore, I had to be strategic in how I handled these situations, balancing expectations of professionalism, my personal politics, and the well-being of my Black girl interlocutors. The Black girls at Liberty Prep would have to navigate this environment even after I concluded my participant-observation, so I did not want to intervene in incendiary ways that would potentially make things worse for them in my absence. Instead of confronting Liberty Prep staff directly, I tried to mitigate the hostility directed at Black girls as much as possible by creating a collaborative, affirmative classroom environment, celebrating students' accomplishments, allowing the girls to share stories or have chat sessions, and mediating when the girls had conflicts with specific staff members.

In addition to interpersonal relations, assigning grades comprised the other main ethical challenge that came with doing participant observation as a volunteer teacher. Teacher-student relationships have an inherent power discrepancy in which grading practices and policies play a significant role. Related to grading policies, I had to ensure that girls understood that their grade for the course, which would appear in their school records, had no correlation to their participation in (any part of) the research. To minimize the power differential associated with grading as much as possible, I solicited the girls' input about the types of digital technologies they enjoyed using, potential discussion topics, their hobbies, and their values. Using their feedback, I developed assignments that would satisfy the curricular expectations of an elective class while honoring the importance of the girls' participation in this research. The girls showed enthusiasm for completing assignments they had a role in creating. To assess their work, I used a labor-based system; as long as girls completed all of the assignments and consistently contributed to class discussions, they earned an A. Both the girls' involvement in shaping course content and the labor-based grading system helped allay the ethical challenges surrounding grade assignments for research participants.

Overall, self-reflexivity has been an essential component of establishing trust with Black girls. During the recruitment process, several girls seemed surprised by my genuine interest in their lives. Explaining to my research participants that I wanted to learn from them contradicted the top-down, didactic interactions with adults to which they had likely grown accustomed. The establishment of horizontal communication with research participants demonstrated a prioritization of Black girls' humanity, which many of them had not experienced in their relationships with adults in institutions. I showed Black girls I valued them and, in turn, they entrusted me with their stories.

You Don't Know Me Like That: Black Girls' Privacy in Digital Publics

Issues of privacy lie at the heart of digital ethics. Both academic and popular discourses of online privacy place significant emphasis on how corporations store, sell, and manipulate digital data. While these concerns rightfully take up space in conversations and policies, the impact of identity categories on privacy (or lack thereof) deserves more attention as a matter of digital ethics. Racialized digital practices and phenomena such as digital blackface, racist social media algorithms, racially biased facial recognition, and digital criminalization raise ethical questions regarding everyday digital technologies and exchanges.[8] These identity-based concerns complicate a strict public/private binary when it comes to online content because of the disproportionately negative consequences privacy breaches can have on marginalized people. For Black girls specifically, public/private binaries do not adequately account for Black girls' positions within the paradox of hyper(in)visibility or the ways that scrutiny of Black girls tempers their privacy in ways beyond their control.[9] Therefore, the particular ethical dilemmas that emerge at the intersection of Black girlhood and public or private digital content require consideration of the extent to which public digital content should be shared outside of the platforms where it originally appeared.

Deciding whose accounts to access was one of the first decisions I had to make regarding research design and implementation. Most of the popular social media applications have privacy settings that allow users to determine whether their content is public or private.[10] In social media language, a public account means anyone who visits the user's page can see all the content they have posted on their profile. Private accounts require permission from the user to view (some or all) the contents of the account. The process for obtaining this permission comes in the form of sending requests ("friend" requests on Facebook and "follow" requests on apps like Instagram, Twitter, and Snapchat). The designation of an account as private is somewhat misleading because a person who has access to private accounts can take screenshots and share them with others who have not been granted permission. Additionally, social media sites often sell data to third parties, and they can be compelled to turn over data to law enforcement. The IRB, which functions as the ethical authority on digital academic research, uses these already fraught definitions of privacy within digital spaces to establish parameters of public and private digital content. For instance, at the time I started this research, the required IRB training presented any publicly available social media content as fair game for data collection, analysis, and sharing.

Using the IRB requirements as a guideline, I only collected screenshots and link information from public social media accounts for the virtual ethnography portion of my research. I maintained a digital chart of these screenshots, links to the profile pages, notes about the content, and my analyses of the images. By using the links, instead of simply following public accounts, I could tell if a girl switched her account to private, at which point I would make a note to ensure I did not share specific quotes or information from her profile. While I only collected images and links from public accounts on Instagram, YouTube, and Snapchat, during in-person conversations with groups of girls, some of them invited me to follow them on Instagram. Therefore, some parts of the overall analysis reflect observations from private accounts. For example, in highlighting image genres, I note motifs that appeared in my perusal of Black girls' digital content, but these descriptions are general and do not allude to specific details from private accounts.

Even publicly available accounts raise ethical questions about maintaining confidentiality and anonymity. The IRB did not require name changes or anonymity for users with public accounts—even when these users are children. While the IRB considers children a vulnerable group, Black girls' susceptibility to harm is more pronounced in a society that rarely grants them the same compassion as their white counterparts. Black girls' experiences of harassment and exploitation online necessitated taking steps beyond the IRB's requirements.[11] Therefore, throughout the book, I do not use girls' real names or real screen names, even for public accounts (except in chapter 4 to give credit to Black girls engaging in activist work).

(Re)evaluating online privacy through a Black girlhood lens helped elucidate distinct ethical dilemmas that arise when researching (with) Black girls in digital spaces. I wanted to protect Black girls as much as possible from potential harm caused by ethical slippages around audience (both intended and actual) and unintended responses and reactions. My attention to Black girls' privacy in digital spaces demonstrates respect for the spaces they have created for themselves.

Representing Black Girls

Along with addressing ethical questions while in the process of ethnographic data collection, I also had to think through the ethics of presenting what I had learned from Black girls about their (digital) lives. From 2015 to 2020, I took screenshots of thousands of images from Black girls' social media accounts. According to fair use copyright rules, these screenshots of publicly available, noncopyrighted content from social media can be printed in published work. However, much like the IRB guidelines, fair use does not always capture the complexities of Black representation. The visual field can be a tricky place for Black girls to navigate, especially under the gaze(s) of misogynoir. While Black girls certainly have no responsibility to appease this oppressive gaze, they still absorb the material and discursive harms that result from (oftentimes intentional) misreading of their visual representation(s). The potential influences of visual representation on Black girls' lived experiences added another ethical layer to choices about how to show Black girls' digital content.

To balance issues of representation and gaze with the realities of my positionality and concern for Black girls' privacy, this book depicts illustrations of Black girls instead of original screenshots of their digital content. Even though teens post images to social media accounts that are set to public, they may not want their photos and videos floating around outside the digital platforms where they originally posted them. Relatedly, using illustrations, instead of the original photos and videos, accounts for when girls turn their accounts from public to private and when they delete certain images. People have many reasons for changing the content on their social media profiles, so I want to respect those decisions by not circulating photos or video screenshots that girls have taken off the internet for whatever reason. Finally, illustrations provide some protection of research participants' identities because the illustrations have enough differences in facial and bodily likenesses to protect the original users' confidentiality. Furthermore, illustrations make it harder for people to do a reverse image lookup. These characteristics of illustrations help to assuage ethical challenges related to Black girls' visual representation.

The process for selecting which illustrations to include combined my affective responses to the girls' images and how they help to advance the arguments the text makes about Black girls' digital practices. I also wanted the images to reflect the diversity of Black girls in terms of complexion, body size, demeanor, etc. After deciding which images to use, I had to decide on an illustrator. Although talent played an integral role in the search for an illustrator, the choice also reflected my philosophical and political commitments. I did not want the illustrations to be constructed from a male gaze. Additionally, the illustrations needed to look realistic to convey the seriousness of Black girls' lives and experiences. I reached out to a few people, and Al Valentín, a Boricua, nonbinary New Yorker, emerged as the right person to visualize Black girls' lives through illustration for this project. From a personal, anecdotal standpoint, Valentín and I have been friends for years. We met as members of the same doctoral student cohort and have bonded over our shared research interests coupled with occasional dabbling in *bonchinche*. As a scholar, Valentín focuses on digital media, gaming, and race and spends time grappling with issues of representation and the gaze. Based on our personal connection along with Valentin's intellectual commitments, I knew they would create the illustrations with a sense of care and respect for Black girls. Throughout the creative process, Valentín sent samples, which allowed us to have conversations about what the images should convey aesthetically and affectively. Therefore, the illustrations that appear in this book reflect a careful engagement with ethical questions about Black girlhood representation.

Ultimately, the choice to include illustrations of Black girls reflects how Black girl autopoetics (BGA) as theory (re)shapes digital ethics. Applying BGA to digital ethics centers processes and consequences of racialization in digital spaces and practices. Additionally, the use of illustrations of Black girls' digital content helps further establish considerations for ethical visualization(s) of Blackness that help paint a fuller picture of Black life without reducing Blackness to spectacle. BGA helps address ongoing concerns about the ethical portrayal of Blackness.

Conclusion: Toward Black Girl Digital Ethics

Evaluating ethical issues within the context of Black girlhood(s) proved generative beyond implementing a digital ethics framework. For one, this BGA-inspired version of digital ethics adds to conversations about the role of the IRB in interdisciplinary humanities work. In researching for this book, I could not help noticing the persistent idea of so-called pure humanities inquiry as I frequently received pushback from some more senior scholars about using ethnography for a humanities project. For these people, humanities methods, except for oral histories, should be limited to texts and not include living people. This book asserts the methodological flexibility of humanities research. Additionally, the book reiterates the notion that ethics is not a universally applied concept; identity matters in establishing ethical frameworks. Of course, there is an ethical baseline for research, especially when dealing with human participants, and the IRB offers a solid foundation for doing ethically sound research with vulnerable populations. However, even with these additional protections, there are layers of vulnerability shaped by identity categories. These layers must be taken seriously and incorporated into research methodologies to ensure the highest ethical standards. While none of these conversations are new, BGA recenters them in ways that hopefully shape future research for the better.

Places to Be
*Black Girls Mapping, Navigating, and
Creating Space through Digital Practice*

1

I never set out to be a high school teacher. My grandmother was a teacher. My mom was a teacher's assistant. Both of my maternal aunts were teachers (though one of them eventually became a social worker), and even my oldest brother spent a year teaching GED classes to young adults. But at twenty-one years old, my level of planning did not match my level of ambition. So instead of moving to Europe and completing a master's degree in media studies at the University of Amsterdam, where I had been accepted (but without the big, prestigious scholarship for international students), I found myself back home in Kinston, North Carolina, after I finished my undergraduate studies. I had about seven dollars to my name and no viable leads for employment.

In a moment of serendipity, one of my childhood friends, whom I'd lost contact with for some time, found herself back in Kinston after graduation as well. We reconnected, and she told me that she planned to apply for teaching jobs in our local school system while she figured out her next career move. I decided to try the same thing since my "backup plan" to move to New York City was not panning out either.[1] We both got jobs teaching that year: she started a position at a middle school working in special education, and I got hired as an English teacher at the same high school I attended for ninth and tenth grades. In fact, the classroom where I taught was the same exact classroom where I took World Geography in tenth grade.

Even though I had veered far from my original postundergraduate plan, as the school year approached, I became excited to be in a job that I felt would allow me to serve my home community in a meaningful way. That excitement lasted for less than a week. On the first Friday at my new job, I was delivering a lesson in my tenth-grade English class. In the ten seconds that I turned around to write something on the board, a fight broke out between two students, one of whom was at least twice my size, and I froze. Another student, who had become unfortunately all too familiar with the eruption of classroom fights, called 221 (the number to the main office) and told them there was a fight. I used that number so many times during my nine months at that school, but the time that solidified my decision to leave happened on a cold morning right before the end of the first semester. By that time, I knew the signs of escalation, so when the two students started ignoring my requests for them to get back to work, I called 221. I explained that a verbal altercation was escalating, and that I needed assistance to prevent a full-on fight. The person who answered the phone told me, "Call back when there is an actual fight," and hung up. Of course, the two students started fighting. I called back for help, and no one came for ten minutes. By the time the resource officer got there, the students had done significant damage to each other and the classroom itself. I finished out the year to avoid breaching my contract, but I submitted my resignation for the next year without having any prospects lined up for the future. I vowed to myself I would never teach at the K–12 level again.

Two years later at the end of my master's degree program, in some ironic sort of déjà vu, I found myself with unstable employment, which put me on the verge of eviction. In the long hours I spent scouring the web for a full-time job, I stumbled upon an advertisement for an English and history teaching fellowship at an all-girls private school in Richmond, Virginia, the city that had become my home while I pursued graduate education. The salary was meager, but the position came with free housing, so I applied.

I could not have predicted that filling out that one job application would lead me down a path to learn more about Black girls' digital practices, especially because the school was not a particularly Black (or Black-friendly) space. In fact, I spent the first two or three weeks in my new position feeling guilty about teaching at this privileged school instead of teaching in communities with more Black children, but my sense of guilt eventually turned into an epiphany about the role of Black faculty members in predominantly white educational settings. My first classroom was in the basement of the school's main building. There were windows, but they only looked out to the concrete structures of the first floor. To say that I did not like the location of my classroom at first would be an understatement, but it became a somewhat sacred space for the students who frequented it. In that first year, I had three Black students—all in the same section of ninth-grade English. One of them ended up becoming my advisee, and the other two visited my classroom enough that I acted as an unofficial advisor and "school mom" for them as well;[2] they came to my classroom at least once a day outside of instructional time, and they continued this visitation long after they moved on from ninth grade. While I expected to have and maintain connections with students in my classes, I began to notice that Black girls I didn't even teach would come visit me in my classroom at least a few times a week—sometimes multiple times in one day.

I should note that girls of diverse racial and ethnic backgrounds frequented my basement classroom.[3] I taught ninth grade, which is a critical period of transition, and many students found my laid-back, nurturing approach comforting. But the Black girls' visits were specific to their experiences as Black girls; their reasons for needing to be comforted or consoled or calmed down were different from their non-Black peers. Not only were their motivations for visiting me different from the other girls', but they had a specific manner of visiting. For instance, the Black girls almost always closed the door when they came in to talk to me, especially if they wanted to talk about something unrelated to class or school. Another difference is that they would almost always visit in pairs or groups, and they kept their voices low oftentimes, which led me to think of my classroom as a kind of hush harbor for the school's Black girls.

In addition to functioning as a hush harbor of sorts, my basement classroom served as a space where these Black girls could be unrestricted in their Blackness. All of our conversations did not reflect frustration. In fact, my classroom became a place where we would talk about the latest music, watch funny YouTube videos, dance, and laugh at memes.[4] While all these lighthearted interactions helped cultivate a bond between the girls and me, their interest in a new social media application, Snapchat, drove me to develop a deeper understanding of their lives. The year—2010—I started working at this school was the same year that Snapchat launched, and the app became a common topic of conversation during our hush harbor sessions, but the girls would never actually let me see anything they posted to their accounts. When I juxtaposed this kind of open secrecy that they maintained in our interactions to the stories they would share with me about the racism of their peers (and sometimes their teachers), I began to wonder about the role of Snapchat—and social media applications more broadly—in offering ways for Black girls to have spaces where they could be themselves, where they could simply *be* without having to worry about someone calling them loud or someone walking past a group of them and asking, "What are you up to?"⁵ In making these connections and asking these nascent questions, I had not yet considered how digital spaces replicate face-to-face oppressive forces. Instead, I observed how the girls laughed with each other when they talked about their Snapchat adventures, and I wondered how this digital space might be providing an additional space akin to my classroom that allowed them to just be.

That teaching (and bonding) experience solidified my ties to Richmond, inspiring me to return to have more conversations with Black girls outside of my own philosophical musings. My ethnographic research included participant observation, discussion groups, and informal conversations. The participant observation involved volunteer teaching at a high school in Richmond's East End, which I refer to as Liberty Prep. For the discussion groups, I met with two small groups of Black girls who attended various middle and high schools throughout Richmond. During the sessions we discussed the kinds of things these girls like to post on social media, what draws them to certain platforms, and what they want people to know about them based on their social media posts. In addition to these formal methods, I met with a Black girl affinity group at an independent school in Richmond (which I refer to as West Academy) where I served as a guest speaker for one of their monthly meetings.

Using these experiences in Richmond as a case study, this chapter explores the space-making components of Black girl autopoetics (BGA). I argue that Black girls' digital content functions as a map of the interconnected, multilayered spatialities they must navigate and create in ongoing processes of self-development and meaning-making. The title of this chapter operates as a double entendre: On one level it gestures to the colloquial phrase "I have places to be," meaning places to go. On the second level, it identifies how Black girls create places where they can *be*, meaning where they can *exist* in ways that conduce their subjective formation and expression.

It's Levels to This: Black Girls' Multilayered Geographies

Black feminist approaches to geography highlight space-making as a central and necessary component of Blackness.⁶ Given the inextricability of Blackness and geography, grappling with Black girls' relationships to space is crucial to understanding how Black girlhood operates. Black girl cartographers, to use Tamara T. Butler's term, theorize space as intrinsically multidimensional and porous, meaning spaces that Black girls occupy, navigate, and create "[unsettle] the colonial project of mapping and [move] us away from flat dimensions of boundary setting."⁷ In alignment with geographical analyses that understand

Black girls' spatialities as collective, creative, transformative, and subversive, BGA not only provides a means to "[expand] Black spatial possibilities" but also evinces how (Black girls') geographies are multilayered: traversing physical, conceptual, and digital spaces.[8]

When I refer to physical space in the chapter, this includes cities and their topographies (land, buildings, waterways, etc.). These are spaces that touch the physical body and/or spaces where people experience the physicality of their bodies. In the United States, couplings of restrictions and over-policing often characterize Black girls' physical worlds. While most American children are subject to restrictions on their movement in public spaces, the perceived transgression of these restrictions have dire material consequences—such as suspension and expulsion from school—for Black girls.[9] Even outside of school contexts, Black girls (and women) who are seen as inappropriately occupying public spaces are subject to physical violence at rates much higher than their white counterparts.[10]

Inextricably linked to Black girls' experiences of the physical, conceptual space refers to worldviews and self-perceptions. To explain conceptual space, I draw from LaKisha Simmons's theorization of mental mapping. In her discussion of Black children growing up in segregated New Orleans, Simmons explains how Black children developed mental maps, which were "multi-layered and fragmented . . . conceptual scales of the city and its buildings, streets, ecology, play areas, and people imperfectly meshed together."[11] Unlike many standard geographical maps, "children's mental maps are not to scale, nor do they correspond neatly with cartographers' mappings of the city. Instead, they reflect children's own experiences, their cognitive development, and their growing sense of the world around them."[12] In my explanation of Black girls' spatial layers, conceptual space comprises the terrain of the mental map. The conceptual space blends memory, knowledge, and meaning-making where Black girls store what they have learned and use these lessons to inform how they move through their worlds.

The other layer of space that I discuss in this chapter is digital space, which includes the internet and technological platforms—such as social media—whose functionality relies on internet affordances. In my conceptualization of the digital, space is not a metaphor, as the internet contains visual and textual content that both has its own materiality and re-presents the materiality of its subjects.[13] In addition to the presence of material content, how people use the digital also determines its spatiality. For instance, the use of social media to establish networks constitutes one way in which digital spatiality manifests. While early champions of digital utopias viewed using the internet as a disembodied experience, digital spaces do not transcend embodiment; instead, embodiment registers differently in digital spaces than it does in physical spaces. Therefore, Black girls' experiences in online social networks mirror their embodied experiences (of racism, sexism, homophobia, etc.). In this way, Black girls' digital worlds are not free from limitations, but digital spaces allow for different kinds of movement.

Following the logic of Black and feminist theorizations of geography that often "treat space as a dynamic constellation of material relations, structural processes, ideologies, and bodily relations," Black girls' digital, physical, and conceptual worlds merge together.[14] Their digital content and practices not only demonstrate how these spaces overlap but also render the borders within digital, physical, and conceptual fictitious, which, in turn, further falsifies the dichotomy between online and in real life (IRL). The spatial nature of Black girlhood allows Black girls to exercise their creativity as space-makers, forcing them to make critical decisions about which spaces they should or should not enter and how to best navigate precarious, yet unavoidable, spaces. These acts of mapping speak to both the multidimensionality and fluidity of Black girls' geographies. Attending to complexities of Black girls' spatialities is essential to positioning them as theorists within discourses of Black girlhood.

Mapping Black Girlhood

In this section, I use excerpts of conversations that I had with groups of Black girls to show how they use BGA to engage in processes of mapping.[15] These maps are simultaneously digital, physical, and conceptual. My articulation of mapping here draws from the aforementioned premise of mental mapping but differs slightly in its placement and construction of the map. Mental mapping combines the conceptual and physical worlds by using narrative, experiences, and memory to avoid dangerous places. For instance, LaKisha Simmons uses the concept of mental mapping to talk about how Black girls in segregated New Orleans navigated the city. While mental mapping fuses the conceptual (what girls come to learn about the world) with the physical (how they literally move through a city), these mental maps have no concrete manifestation. By adding the digital layer, Black girls' posts on social media (and other internet sites) become material evidence of (1) how they navigate and create space(s) and (2) the overlap of the physical, conceptual, and digital. While the dangers that Black girls face in all these spatial dimensions are certainly not new, their engagement with the digital offers more insight into how they identify and try to avoid or cope with these ever-present threats.

Liberty Prep: A Culture of Discipline

Of the places I observed in Richmond, I spent the most time at a high school working with a small group of Black girls at Liberty Preparatory School (hereby referred to as Liberty Prep) in Richmond's East End.[16] Each morning on my drive to Liberty Prep, I encountered the shift in neighborhoods—a phenomenon that happens in many urban cities where one street separates a highly sought-after neighborhood from parts of the city where local residents warn out-of-towners not to go. Driving into the East End from downtown Richmond, one can see the abrupt transition from university buildings, shops, and posh condominiums to abandoned lots, run-down houses, and convenience stores. The East End is an area of concentrated poverty—with four of the city's six housing projects located in this neighborhood.[17] Despite a growing number of gentrifiers, many of the houses in the neighborhood remain in desperate need of work and renovations that their occupants cannot afford. In the unoccupied houses, grass and weeds grow high and wild—a sight you rarely see in the West End. The neighborhood has an abundance of corner stores, where residents can buy liquor, lottery tickets, and fried food, but few grocery stores.[18] The East End is also a high crime density area; in 2020 when overall crime statistics for the city had decreased, shootings in the East End increased, especially after the COVID-19 stay-at-home orders ended for Virginia.[19]

In many ways, Liberty Prep embodies the sociocultural dynamics of East End high schools, in terms of both its location and physical surroundings and the demographics of the students. Liberty Prep is a small, two-story building located squarely within a residential neighborhood. There are houses and apartments in immediate walking distance from the school but no places for students who might be running late to grab a quick meal or snack. The school's main doors of entry and exit remained locked at all times; visitors had to wait outside until one of the school's designated adult staff came to open the door. At the building's entrance, the administrators had a table set up in the foyer, not a front office, where visitors could sign in (and out) and where they required students to place their cell phones (in a bin) before attending the morning assembly. Three small classrooms lined the hallway leading to the cafeteria, the assigned gathering place for students in the morning. The second floor housed more classrooms along with a modest computer lab and administrative offices. As far as Liberty Prep's population, during the time I was there, all of the students were Black and from low-income households. The school personnel were mostly white, though there were two Black male administrators, and only one staff member lived in the East End. However, Liberty Prep differed from the area schools in other ways. It was much smaller than many other schools in the area, with fewer than one hundred students in the whole school. On the one hand, this small number created more optimal classroom sizes where students could get more focused instruction. On the other hand, this small size created more opportunities for school personnel to infringe upon students' privacy and autonomy. Liberty Prep's utilization of volunteers to supplement their small teaching staff marked another key difference from other schools in the area.[20] Because of the school's small size, the salaried teachers taught core subjects such as English, math, science, history, and foreign languages while volunteers covered some elective courses.[21]

During my time living in Richmond, I became involved with a few organizations in the city's East End. I decided to conduct part of my research at Liberty Prep partially because of these community ties. Additionally, Liberty Prep's volunteer structure seemed like an ideal opportunity to get to know some Black girls in the area without applying for an extra job. I emailed the head of school, Joyce, and informed her about my interest in volunteering at Liberty Prep. She let me know that they had enough volunteers for the after-school program, but they needed some volunteers to teach electives. My first meeting with Joyce, a white woman, offered a preview of the challenges I would face as a researcher in this particular school environment. During our conversation, Joyce recalled a field trip where Liberty Prep students went to a basketball game at Hampton University, located about an hour east of Richmond in the Hampton Roads region of Virginia. When reflecting upon the students' behavior, Joyce noted her surprise that students weren't more excited to attend a basketball game at a historically black college or university (HBCU). She attributed their subdued, timid behavior to the fact that "they were not used to being around Black people who weren't acting 'hood.'"[22] I suppressed my shock at the nonchalance with which she made that statement. In fact, I became even more eager to talk to Black girls in the school because I wanted to both learn more about students' experiences from their own perspectives and affirm that whatever their affinities to the "hood" might be, they are no less worthy of a supportive school environment.

Both the meeting with Joyce and the presentation I gave to the rest of the faculty about my proposed course seemed to foreshadow the conflict between my goals as an advocate for Black girls and the school's role as a disciplinary institution. In my presentation, I described the course I planned to teach, Digital Expressions, and explained that the goal of the course would be to learn about how the girls experienced their digital environments. We would talk about things they valued in constructing their online identities and the ways they interacted with others online. Even though I never said anything about the class being a proscriptive lesson in what to post and not post online, several faculty members commented about how they appreciated having someone come talk to the girls about appropriate online behavior. Their comments revealed their damning assumptions about the nature of Black girls' digital practices and how they saw the digital as another area that needed to be policed by school personnel, especially when it comes to Black girls.

Despite the clear differences between my vision and the school's, Joyce approved me to teach Digital Expressions as an elective. I started in August 2016. In my class, I had five girls—two ninth graders and three twelfth graders. My original plan for the class was to create a collaborative archive using photographs that the girls would have submitted from their social media accounts. These assignments, which I called "photo assignments" in our course syllabus, reflected different themes that the girls identified as important. The process that I used to determine the assignment themes involved asking the girls to write a paragraph describing information or topics they would want to include in an online archive about themselves. I put the girls' paragraphs into a word cloud, an online application that visualizes the most frequently used words in a given piece of writing by making those words bigger than other words in the text. Based on the word cloud results, the girls expressed the most interest in the following topics: self, history or heritage, art, Richmond, community, family, girlhood, favorite things, dreams, and travel. Even though the girls came up with these excellent themes, my vision for the class and collaborative approach did not work out for several reasons. First, students at Liberty Prep did not choose their own electives. Instead, the guidance counselor scheduled them for classes based on core class offerings and the core teachers' schedules. While I was able to make sure that the counselor only put girls in the course, that was the extent of my control. So the girls enrolled in Digital Expressions did not know anything about the course until the first day of class, and they might not have chosen it over other options.[23] Second, I overestimated the girls' ability to apply the skills they employed in creating content for social media to more formal digital assignments like building a website or making a photo essay. Therefore, I had to adjust the final products that came from the class. I would have preferred to have students who signed up for the class out of interest, and I could have designed more lessons teaching the girls how to build websites.[24] However, the compulsory enrollment and lack of tech skills did not form the biggest barrier to understanding the girls' digital practices—it was the school environment itself.

As a whole, the disciplinary practices at Liberty Prep were not unique; restrictive policies regarding dress, cell phones, lunch times, and students' overall existence are a hallmark of K–12 education in the United States, and Black students are subject to more unfair and disproportionate policing than their white counterparts. Breaking these statistics down even further to look at gender, disciplinary actions for Black girls often correspond to school administrators' perceptions of them transgressing appropriate boundaries of femininity by being too loud, too aggressive, or too unpleasant.[25] The disciplinary actions that I saw (or heard about secondhand from the girls in Digital Expressions) at Liberty Prep usually fell in line with a policing of femininity.

Oftentimes before class started, the Digital Expressions girls would have conversations about their weekends or other time outside of school. As seniors, Kim and Jennifer both had jobs. One day, the two girls were talking about the different tasks they do at work, and Jennifer, whose voice carries naturally, started describing how people smeared feces on the walls and left used tampons on the floor in the bathroom at her job. When she made the comment about tampons, a female teacher walked into my classroom uninvited to tell Jennifer that other teachers could hear her, including one of the male teachers. The teacher said that her male colleague probably did not feel comfortable hearing about tampons. Jennifer responded, "Well he is going to have a daughter one day," indicating that she didn't see any reason why he should be uncomfortable hearing the word "tampons." The teacher responded, "Well regardless, you are in school, so act professional." For K–12 learners, school is not a profession. Furthermore, it is clear from the invocation of the male teacher's potential discomfort that "professional" in this context was code for "ladylike."

Another representative example of policing femininity at Liberty Prep occurred when Destiny wore a grill—a metal, sometimes gem-encrusted covering that goes over the teeth—to school. Because of grills' association with hip-hop, and male rappers specifically, wearing a grill falls outside the purview of respectable feminine presentation for those who subscribe to strict, binary gender norms. One of the white female teachers walked by my classroom and saw Destiny showing off her grill. She came in, also uninvited, and told Destiny to take it out because it was "unbecoming." She then tried to insult Destiny by saying that the grill "looked like a bubblegum wrapper that someone stepped on." Destiny refused to take it out—partially because this teacher had no authority over her in *my* classroom. After failing to make her point, the teacher turned to me and said, "Don't let her wear that." I didn't respond to her, but when she left, I told the girls, "Y'all know I'm not gonna make her take her grill out." They all laughed, and Kim said, "Right. Because it's her mouth." Kim's comment speaks to the ways in which policing femininity attempts to strip girls of their (bodily) autonomy. They felt like this teacher should not be concerned about Destiny's bodily adornments and recognized the reprimand for its true intent: policing. It is important to note that Destiny's grill did not violate the school's dress code (which is already inherently sexist). Instead, this teacher took personal offense to Destiny's grill because it represented a transgression of docile femininity.

In a somewhat passing conversation, one of the administrators, Oliver, mentioned to me that the "young ladies just can't seem to get it together." He had hinted at the girls not behaving like "ladies" before, and his comments solidified how even benign behavior gets characterized as malicious when it does not conform to a certain standard of so-called ladylike behavior. While teachers' comments leveled at Jennifer and Destiny and Oliver's offhand remarks might seem like isolated instances of nitpicking, a structure of policing Black girls' bodies and behaviors enabled all of these individual actions. The girls' own assessment of policing and discipline around dress code demonstrates how systemic misogynoir undergirded the school's everyday operations. Over the course of the semester I spent with the girls in Digital Expressions, school dress codes came up frequently as a topic of discussion and critique. For example, Destiny's recollection of a time she broke dress code reveals her discontent with the rules but also how the rules conflicted with her own sense of identity: "Mrs. Wade, I wore this crop top here.... It was in the summer. And it didn't even show my whole entire stomach, and I got looked at like I was being grown, but I won't!! And they were about to make me change. Every time I wear something, they always gotta be like, 'That's too short' or 'You bein' grown.' I'm not." When Destiny relayed her story, Kim began to reflect on a similar experience.

> Yeah, when I was in tenth grade, I had wore, like, this skirt, and I had wore, like, this crop top or whatever, but you couldn't see no stomach. My skirt, it was, like, high enough that it came up over my whole stomach. The shirt was just a little short. But when I came in Mr. Oliver was like—because I guess he knew what kinda shirt it was even though he couldn't see nothin'—he was like, "Oh no!" He was like, "Reach to the Lord." I guess because if I do like this [raises her hands up] my shirt will come up, but I'm not gonna do like this! So, my shirt's not gonna come up.

I told the girls that I understood their situations and explained the prejudices in school dress codes, which led to a conversation about inconsistencies in dress code enforcement based on body size. Jennifer interjected: "Like, if [a thinner classmate] was to wear leggings, they wouldn't say nothing to her, but I wore leggings one day, and they said something to me. Is it because I'm fat? You're discriminating!"

While these complaints about dress code might seem insignificant or like the girls merely want to justify breaking the rules, they actually highlight the racialized and gendered biases embedded in these rules in the first place. The girls' insistence on the dress code's unfair nature reflects more than an empty complaint or expression of dissatisfaction—it reflects the dissonance between how they understand themselves as human beings with dignity and how dress codes not only render them objects of scrutiny but also lead the adults around them to draw inaccurate conclusions about their character that have a material impact on how they experience the school environment.

Furthermore, telling girls to act like ladies presents a host of problems, including, but certainly not limited to, adultification, potential misgendering, and imposition of respectability. Girls are not "ladies in training." They are children. Children should be allowed to explore their values and identities without adults imposing gender norms on them. The other disturbing thing about these incidences of policing is that they occurred in the form of interruptions to my class. I found people's audacity to walk in my classroom to correct my students' behavior appalling and offensive, and I suspect that the frequent interruptions had a direct connection to my embodiment as a Black woman and a refusal to run my class as a disciplinary space. Before teaching at Liberty Prep, I had five years of experience teaching high school students, so I could identify dangerous or problematic behaviors easily. None of my students exhibited those behaviors. But because they were "too loud" or "too crude," other staff members perceived me as not being able to manage my class and felt the need to step in to help. If that type of behavior made *me* upset over a period of six months, imagine what girls attending the school for four years have to do to cope.

Navigating Power Discrepancies

The administrators' policing of the girls at Liberty Prep was consistently accompanied by threats—of failing grades, suspension, or expulsion. The experiences of two girls, Stacey and Kim, exemplify the severity of the school's police-and-threaten culture. Stacey was a bright, outspoken senior who often expressed her frustrations with the administrative staff at Liberty Prep. About a week into the semester, Stacey came to class one morning upset about yet another threat to kick her out, explaining that Joyce told her that she would take "extreme steps" to remove her from the school. A few days after Stacey made this complaint, Joyce suspended her, and I—along with her other teachers—received an email stating she had been suspended because she was having problems with authority, which, according to Joyce and other staff, had been a problem since she began the school in ninth grade. Instinctively, and as a Black girlhood scholar, I already understood what had happened to Stacey. Oftentimes when Black girls demonstrate a sense of confidence and self-worth, people, especially white people and Black men, characterize them as attitudinal. Despite my intuitive sense of Stacey's situation, I decided to schedule a meeting with Joyce to get an understanding of what everyone else seemed to dislike about Stacey that I simply did not see in my interactions with her. During our meeting, Joyce explained that Stacey showed "excessive pride" and needed to practice "humility." She went on to say that Stacey shuts down anytime things don't go her way, and that her attitude "is going to keep her in poverty." The racism embedded in this assessment of Stacey is astounding. What does it mean for a Black girl to have "excessive pride" in a sociopolitical context that so often violates and erases Black girls, and then to be punished for that pride? In addition to trying to discipline Stacey into humility, Joyce framed the decision to suspend her as helping her because, as she put it, without humility, Stacey would stay in poverty. Unfortunately, this lack of systemic acknowledgment and analysis is not limited to Joyce or Liberty Prep, and it is detrimental to Black girls (and Black children in general) when educators and other people working with youth believe that the children's individual choices *alone* will be the difference between staying in poverty or making it out. To be clear, I do not mean to suggest that Black girls, or Black children in general, should be exempt from following school rules. Instead, I invoke Stacey's story to point out how anti-Blackness, specifically misogynoir, influences the establishment and enforcement of school rules.

Shortly after Stacey came back to school, she had another altercation with an administrator, Oliver. Some mornings when I got to campus early enough, I saw Oliver standing in the foyer greeting students as they arrived. As part of this greeting, he would require students to look him in the eyes and shake his hand. When Stacey's turn came to greet him, she said "Good morning" but did not shake Oliver's hand. He made her keep walking back outside and redo the greeting until she finally gave in to his request for a handshake. As the ordeal played out, she noticed me watching and turned to me and mouthed, "See?" She wanted me to witness the source of her incessant frustration, and I did. Oliver's behavior was problematic not only because he singled Stacey out but also because of the message that his interaction sends to girls: if an adult man wants to make physical contact with you, you are required to honor his requests, and if not, suffer the consequences. Stacey was absolutely justified in pushing back against a petty rule that requires her to make physical contact with adults. Educators do not have any entitlement to their students' bodies. Stacey did not stay at Liberty Prep for the whole school year. After about a month of having her in my class, she left to attend another school. While the things that drove her from Liberty Prep amounted to an egregious injustice, she did leave the school on her own terms instead of being expelled.

Unlike Stacey's, Kim's circumstances did not afford her many options beyond Liberty Prep. The other high school in her district is notorious for being an unsafe environment where learning is nearly impossible. In fact, the school has such a bad reputation that Liberty Prep administrators used it as a threat to make students behave, as if threatening to send the students to prison. One morning, Oliver asked me to come sit with him and Kim as they had a conversation about potentially expelling her. A few days earlier, Kim had participated in a prank where she and other students locked a teacher out of her classroom. According to Oliver, all of the other students involved had admitted their wrongdoing and apologized, except Kim. Oliver claimed that since the incident, Kim had become more defiant and had been sent home early one day as a result of her insolent behavior. Oliver gave Kim an ultimatum: she could demonstrate remorse or be sent to the other school in the district. But Kim's demonstration of remorse consisted of her explaining to him why she deserved to stay at Liberty Prep. In other words, she essentially had to beg to stay instead of being placed in another school environment that Oliver knew she would not be able to handle socially. Kim complied because she had a lack of viable options for finishing high school. Oliver saw the exchange as a success. Certainly, Kim should have been held accountable for her actions, but making her beg read as a gross manipulation of power, a type of power flex these girls experienced on a regular basis.

Danger-Zone Management

While Stacey's and Kim's situations serve as specific examples of extreme power imbalances, all the girls in Digital Expressions (and the students at Liberty Prep more broadly) had a keen awareness of the relationship between surveillance and discipline. They attended school in a hypersurveillance environment with a quite invasive administrative approach. Furthermore, the students at Liberty Prep, by virtue of where they lived, had experience with neighborhood surveillance by law enforcement, and so they had seen the consequences of people invading their spaces. I first noticed the spatial overlap between physical, digital, and conceptual in the Digital Expressions girls' responses to surveillance and attempts to avoid punishment. Liberty Prep had a strict cell phone policy that required students to turn their phones off and put them in a bin when entering the school. Students could face disciplinary action for several offenses regarding their cell phones: not turning the cell phones in (this includes forgetting to turn it in), accessing the phone without permission during the school day, and lying about not having a cell phone to prevent turning it in. Because of these rules, I had to ask for girls to have special permission to use their phones in my class for our assignments. When we first started using phones in the classroom, and they had permission to go on Instagram or Snapchat to get content to use in classroom exercises, they pretended they forgot their screen names. At first, I found it quite odd that they would suddenly forget the screen names and passwords they used almost every day, but I quickly realized they were trying to protect their digital spaces and content. In this instance, the cell phone policy in the physical school environment meant that, conceptually, the girls came to associate their cell phones with policing and discipline—at least while they were at school. Administrators may have held students' phones hostage in a bin, but the digital content that they accessed through those phones was safe from authoritative eyes. Therefore, the girls in Digital Expressions were hesitant to access their digital profiles in class because they did not want to compromise the spaces they turned to as an escape.

Once the girls realized that I was not going to try to look at their accounts, they gave up on that strategy, but they were still very careful not to say their screen names (or even their friends' screen names) out loud. After I had been working with these girls for a few months, they did start to show me things on their phones. For instance, Kim would sometimes share funny videos she came across during independent work. Jennifer also showed me a few videos from her Instagram account. They were usually not videos that she had recorded but ones that she liked (meaning she hit the "like" button on the content): hairstyles she wanted to try, a video of a young boy singing at his mother's wedding, and a girl fighting a boy who had pulled her hijab at school. Of all the girls, Jennifer was the most likely to show me videos or pictures on her phone. In all of these instances, even though the girls were sharing with me, they were still careful not to show me anything they had posted but instead posts that appeared in their timelines. The one exception is when Jennifer showed me a picture of a mirror selfie she posted before her first nightclub experience with a friend, and even during this moment of sharing, she only showed me the picture and not any identifying features of her Instagram account.

Despite these infrequent moments of sharing, the girls maintained selectivity around their digital content, especially in relation to school-affiliated adults.

JENNIFER: Just like the lady at [after school]. She told me—she told a couple of us—"I'm gonna make Snapchat add y'all." So, she added me.

I blocked her. I don't want her looking at my snaps. I post inappropriate stuff on there. Not body-wise, but inappropriate that her eyes don't wanna see.

ME: Do you consider her following you an invasion of privacy?

JENNIFER: No. I just don't want her to see.

Jennifer's comments demonstrate a deliberate separation of school and personal life. Through blocking her after-school instructor, Jennifer used digital space to tip the scale of authority toward herself, thus subverting the relationship between student and educator she normally experienced in her physical and conceptual spaces.

In addition to enduring an overly policed environment at school, the girls at Liberty Prep lived in Richmond's East End, which not only has a high overall crime rate but has one of the highest incidences of homicides in the city. The Liberty Prep students living in the neighborhood's housing projects were exposed to a number of shootings, but the violence encompasses a much wider area. The following conversation reflects how at least two of the girls in Digital Expressions processed the violence around them.

STACEY: They always talking about "all lives matter." Every time somebody says "Black lives matter," they are saying "all lives matter—blah, blah blah." So, if all lives matter, then why you ain't helping the Black lives?

KIM: Exactly. It's only Black people that's dying.

Of course, we know other races of people (especially those living in poverty) have been victims of police and vigilante murders. However, for the girls in Digital Expressions, the frequently circulating images of Black death they see online were accompanied by Black death in their own neighborhoods. This overlap between the digital and physical worlds means that conceptually, in these girls' worlds, there *are* only Black people dying. Not only do their social and physical environments shape how the girls perceive campaigns such as Black Lives Matter, but they also influence the girls' ideas about what social media can do materially. After watching a video clip of Michelle Obama speaking to a group on International Women's Day in which she urges young girls to use social media as a tool for social change, I asked the girls in Digital Expressions how they might use social media to make changes in their communities, neighborhoods, schools, or cities.[26] Three out of four girls mentioned violence and how they wanted to change that, but they did not feel optimistic about social media's ability to galvanize people toward such change. One student wrote: "I would change all the black killings (or I would at least try). But people already try to stop the black killings through social media so I don't know if that would really help. But I could like post about all the killings and just talk about it but I don't think that would do anything." This response shows how digital-physical-conceptual spaces merge to create a concept of violence that then shapes digital practices. Even though this student did not feel certainty about the role digital media could play in ending violence in her community, she still sees "post[ing] about the killings" as a potential initial step. The girl's statement presents a sense of inability around changing the physical and conceptual ramifications of community violence. However, in this student's articulation, the digital operates as a means of intervention. Despite the girl's uncertainty about the efficacy of posting about violence online, the digital provides a space to raise awareness, express opinions, and share information about organizing efforts. In this instance, the physical, conceptual, and digital overlap in a way that positions the digital as a space where the girls feel like they can do *something*, even if their actions will not fully address the larger problem.

I do not wish to suggest that the shootings and murders these girls witnessed (either first- or secondhand) resulted mostly from police violence against civilians. Most of the violent crimes that happen in Richmond's East End reflect the kinds of intragroup violence seen in communities that have high concentrations of poverty. However, Stacey's question "Why you ain't helping the Black lives?" illustrates how the girls in my class did not see Black Lives Matter as a statement solely about combatting police and vigilante violence. Instead, they understood the phrase, and its associated movement, as the originators intended: a rallying cry for the protection of Black life from all the forces that seek to eradicate it.

Community violence was not an abstract political or organizing concept for the girls at Liberty Prep. While none of the girls in Digital Expressions shared instances of experiencing firsthand gun violence, their conversations did indicate personal concerns about sexual violence.[27] During one of our early class meetings (within the first week of school), the girls started talking about grown men trying to proposition young girls. One student recalled a time when a man tried to approach her at a gas station; she described his aggression and her annoyance with his advances. The girls discussed this incident in a way that demonstrated both their disgust with predatory men and the frequency with which these types of encounters occurred for them.

This problem of potential sexual harassment and assault also posed a threat among the girls' peers. Jennifer and Kim often stayed after class for a few minutes to talk about everyday high school matters. One day, they were having a conversation about school dances. Jennifer shared that she had been invited to prom and the military ball, but she did not plan to accept either invitation. When Kim asked why, Jennifer said that she did not like either one of the boys. Thinking back to my own senior prom experience—in which my date literally just needed a ticket to the prom; we did not even know each other or hang out at the event—I told them that you do not have to like a boy to go to prom with him. Kim retorted: "Yes, you do! Because they are gonna want to dance, then they gonna want to kiss, then take you home after prom. No. That's dead." Kim's reaction to my statement reflects a general lack of agency and a bit of internalized misogyny she and Jennifer associated with prom, and probably dating in general. Both girls saw accepting an invitation for a date as consenting to letting the date do whatever he wants. In their minds, at least if you like the boy, the sexual advances would be more tolerable.[28]

The digital-physical-conceptual connection between Black girls' potential susceptibility to sexual violence is not always straightforward or clear-cut. On the one hand, girls did use digital spaces to express and explore their sexualities. For instance, Jennifer posted a picture of her nipple ring on Snapchat, and the girls often talked about boys they found attractive with whom they communicated through social media. On the other hand, Jennifer openly expressed concerns about who she allows to follow her on Snapchat and admonished the other girls to do the same: "Like, if you like fifteen and a thirty-year-old man is like, 'Add me on Snapchat,' if that ain't, like, your family or something, it would be creepy. Like, why you wanna add me? I'm too young for you, sweetheart." While these girls' experiences and how they approach sexuality in digital spaces do not constitute a direct "if-then" relationship, the conversations around sex and sexuality still illuminate an overlap of the physical, conceptual, and the digital. The girls had no control over men cat-calling them at the gas station, but they could block these same types of men on social media, thereby preventing the discomfort they experienced in the physical environment. In cases where the girls made or accepted advances from boys via direct messaging on social media, they maintained control over the pace at which these exchanges moved—in contrast to the pressure they felt when going out on dates. Therefore, when it comes to sexuality, the digital functioned as a space to mitigate the aspects of the physical environment beyond the girls' control and facilitate the level of agency they lacked in their conceptual frameworks around dating and consent.

These examples speak to how the Digital Expressions girls navigated their interpersonal interactions, especially within the context of Liberty Prep and

Figure 1.1. Red Cross pool safety poster. Author screenshot.

their neighborhoods, but the spatial overlap between digital, physical, and conceptual also presented itself in how they made sense of concepts like racism and cultural appropriation. During one our early conversations in class, Stacey asked if we had heard of BuzzFeed, which she described as a key source of her lessons about race and feminism.[29] After confirming our familiarity with the platform, Stacey told us about an article BuzzFeed posted calling out racism in a Red Cross poster on pool safety. At the time, the poster (fig. 1.1), which looked almost like a throwback to the 1960s, had gone viral on social media. In her description and summary of the poster, Stacey noted, "[The Red Cross] was saying what to do, what's good, what you're supposed to do, and what you're not supposed to do [at the pool]. And all the bad ones were Black people or minorities. And all the good ones were white people." Stacey understood why the poster was problematic, and she agreed with BuzzFeed's critique, but she quickly became familiar with the racism that lies in the comments: "It'll be people just saying bad stuff.... All the white people in the comments were like, 'They always trying to make stuff [racial]' and basically say it's not a big deal even though it is because the picture is basically trying to say that Black people is wrong and white people are good."

These types of conversations happened frequently as the girls in Digital Expressions processed the kinds of images and discourses they encountered about race and gender (both on and offline). They expressed their frustrations with cultural appropriation and how this phenomenon impacted Black girls and women. After watching an episode of Yaba Blay's "Professional Black Girl" YouTube series, which focuses on Black girls' and women's self-expression through hair, fashion, and other embodied features, we had a discussion about how some people degrade certain Black women's hairstyles or features but praise them when appropriated by other racial or ethnic groups. Jennifer said, "But it's like everybody other than Black people is becoming what Black people are, like what Black people have naturally. Like, the booty, the breasts, all that; lips. They're doing everything that we have, and it's becoming better for them." Jennifer's observation reflects a racist, sexist double standard that punishes Black women when they transgress the bounds of respectable style and presentation while praising and rewarding the same features in white or other non-Black women.[30] Furthermore, Jennifer's assessment that "it's becoming better for them" speaks to the material consequences of cultural appropriation. Jennifer's observations extend beyond an emotional response to highlight how non-Black women have been able to create opportunities for themselves through cultural appropriation.[31]

The physical-digital-conceptual connection that these instances bring to light relates back to how people see Black girls. The Digital Expressions students did not seem to have conceptual hang-ups about their own sense of value based on their encounters with racism and cultural appropriation in digital spaces. In fact, their critiques of these social issues coupled with a refusal to internalize harmful messages about Black girlhood signaled their assurance in knowing they are *not* the problem.[32] However, the blatant racism of the Red Cross poster and the misogynoir undergirding the denigration of Black girls' and women's bodies also shaped the girls' daily interactions. From school administrators seeing a Black girl as being "grown" because she has on a short skirt to grown men catcalling Black girls at gas stations to Black boys feeling like Black girls owe them sex on a date, all of these situations stem from a devaluation of Black girls and women. The behaviors of the girls at Liberty Prep help elucidate how Black girls encounter this devaluation across multiple dimensions of space and how they utilize the overlap of these spaces as a resource that is simultaneously informational and creative.

The Other Side of Town: West Academy and Other Spaces of Personal Development

Even though I spent the majority of my time doing ethnography at Liberty Prep, I had opportunities to interact with other Black girls in noninstructional contexts. First, I visited an affinity group for Black girls at an independent school, West Academy.[33] The group of girls, in grades nine through twelve, met once a month, and their faculty sponsor invited me to be a guest speaker to tell them about college and my research and to have a somewhat informal conversation about their uses of digital media. These girls' experiences differed greatly from the girls at Liberty Prep. For one, the socioeconomic statuses of the girls at West Academy were different from the girls at Liberty Prep. While many of the girls in the group received some form of financial aid from West Academy, their ability to attend the school at all represents a broader set of choices than the ones available to the girls at Liberty Prep. Another big difference between the two groups of girls is the school environment itself. West Academy is in Richmond's West End. Comparing the West End and East End feels like comparing two cities instead of two neighborhoods within the same city. Entering the West End from other neighborhoods requires crossing bridges and/or driving on the Interstate. The West End has an abundance of trees and green spaces, its houses are large and well-maintained, and there's a wealth of grocery stores, shopping squares, and restaurants. Unlike the East End, the West End does not have many bus stops, and police officers rarely patrol the area.

Situated within a residential area known for its million-dollar houses and proximity to exclusive social venues like golf courses and country clubs, West Academy's location exemplifies West End neighborhoods. The school is walking distance from restaurants and shops, which students would frequent during their free periods as well as before and after school. While Liberty Prep's campus consists of a modest two-story building and parking lot, West Academy's campus houses multiple academic buildings, including a well-stocked library, a science building with state-of-the-art labs, and a gym with an Olympic-sized pool. Along with the physical location and neighborhood of West Academy, the school culture fostered and encouraged autonomy (to an extent). Of course, school personnel expected students to be responsible and to follow the established rules outlined in the student handbook. However, features of the school, like its honor code, for example, implied an expectation that students would develop and apply a sense of ethics and integrity. Furthermore, while suspensions and expulsions could, and occasionally did, occur at West Academy, fewer offenses led to these consequences than at schools like Liberty Prep.

Table 1.1. Key differences between Liberty Prep and West Academy

	Liberty Prep	West Academy
Socioeconomic status of students/families	Low-income	Upper-middle class to wealthy
Neighborhood/ surroundings	East End: Corner stores; Heavy police surveillance; High poverty levels; Few parks and green spaces	West End: Plentiful shops, restaurants, and grocery stores; Little-to-no police surveillance; Affluent neighborhood; Several parks and green spaces
School building(s)/ campus features	One campus building with two floors; Laptops available for student use at school only	Several campus buildings, including science building with labs; Separate gym with Olympic-sized pool; Campus library; One-to-one laptop program allowing students to own their computers
School culture	Heavy emphasis on discipline; School uniforms; No cell phones during school day; Frequent suspensions	Rules driven by an honor code; Promotion of autonomy and personal development; Rare suspensions or expulsions

This less tyrannical disciplinary approach meant that the students at West Academy could focus more on intellectual and personal development. West Academy had so many resources that its amenities functioned as a form of behavior management on their own; students would not want to risk getting suspended or expelled and forgo the privilege of accessing such an environment.

In addition to the conversation with girls at West Academy, I held two discussion groups with Black girls: one high school group and one middle school group. The high school group consisted of girls who had graduated from a middle school in the East End designed to change the trajectory of its students' lives. The girls in this discussion group were beneficiaries of a program that creates pathways for their school's graduates to get scholarships and attend a range of independent high schools in Richmond (or, in some cases, boarding schools in other Virginia cities and towns). Despite attending schools in more affluent neighborhoods, the girls from the high school discussion group had a similar socioeconomic status as the girls from Liberty Prep since they all lived in the same East End neighborhood(s). However, their educational experiences more closely mirrored those of the girls at West Academy because their schools had similar approaches to creating learning communities that prioritized personal development over extreme forms of punishment.

The group of middle school girls that conversed with me attended Empowering Black Girls (EBG) summer camp.[34] EBG is run by a nonprofit organization whose mission makes clear that the program welcomes all girls to participate but emphasizes curricular content and enrichment activities that center girls of color, especially Black girls. The environment of EBG reflects its mission of fostering confident, creative Black girls who will make change in their communities. Therefore, the rules that camp participants had to follow did not have the same dictatorial undergirding as a school like Liberty Prep. The lack of an authoritarian environment played a part in how the girls in these spaces understood their relationship to digital/social media.

In contrast to the Liberty Prep girls, the girls that I spoke to at West Academy and the girls in the discussion groups eagerly shared stories about their experiences, and several of them invited me to follow them on social media almost immediately. Both the girls at West Academy and in the discussion groups seemed to get along better with adults than students at Liberty Prep because their relationships to adults in their school and extracurricular and home environments, while not completely devoid of power imbalances, operated under different conditions. However, these amiable relationships did not make the girls at West Academy and the discussion groups any less susceptible to the watchful eyes of adults: they just dealt with (potential) surveillance in different ways.

One of the key factors influencing how the West Academy and discussion group girls understood surveillance had to do with future opportunities, especially attending college. During my conversation with the girls at West Academy, one of them explained how students who had been at West Academy at least since middle school received mandatory training for how to use social media before they could be issued a laptop.[35] During these assembly-style meetings, the computer technology instructor encouraged students to think of social media as an opportunity to brand themselves as well-rounded students in order to garner positive attention from college admissions officers and collegiate athletics personnel. Several of the girls in the group described how they took this advice to heart and used their Instagram pages to curate images of themselves participating in community service and school-sanctioned events. A couple of the girls who were hoping to get athletic scholarships explained how they used their Instagram pages to compile footage from games that would look impressive to scouts and increase their chances of not only attending college but having some or all their expenses paid. Even though the girls in the discussion groups did not have this same formal training and approach to self-branding, they also understood the links between social media and future opportunities. For the group at EBG, they seemed especially concerned (and upset) about the idea of silly things they do as middle schoolers potentially having an impact on their ability to get into college or get a job. Several of the girls cited their awareness of how social media posts can follow a person well into adulthood as a factor that influences what they post. In these instances, the threat of potentially long-lasting consequences shapes the physical-digital-conceptual. What these educational environments lack in terms of physical restriction (like at Liberty Prep) they make up for in conceptual conditioning. In other words, West Academy and the spaces of the discussion groups did not have the same prison-like culture, but the people in authority within these organizations went to great lengths to ensure that the girls understood social media as a space of surveillance. Instead of pushing back against the invasiveness of people scrutinizing the girls' social media accounts, the adults in these girls' lives, understandably, taught them to enact forms of docility by presenting themselves in certain ways online. Therefore, these girls learned to try to avoid consequences altogether by only posting content—at least publicly—that they would be comfortable with their parents, teachers, college admissions officers, and potential employers seeing.

In addition to this surveillance by outsiders, the discussion group and West Academy girls also engaged in a form of peer group scrutiny. One of the girls at EBG, Tory, described a situation where she felt inclined to watch her friends' Snapchat activity because she felt a change in their relationship dynamic. During this period, Tory saw her friends together at a party (to which she did not receive an invitation) on Snapchat, which led to a significant verbal altercation that ended her friendship with that group. Snapchat allows users to send content directly to each other or to post to a broader profile that can be viewed by anyone who accesses the user's account. By posting their attendance at the party in the latter fashion, Tory's former friend group knew she would see them together at the event. For Tory, this post functioned as a reminder of her physical absence from the party, and it was a blow to her conceptualization of girls she thought of as friends. This incident illustrates the imbrication of digital, physical, and conceptual because all the girls involved saw the digital space of Snapchat as an extension of both physical spaces to socialize and the conceptual spaces that determined how they understood their friendship.

Another observation about peer group scrutiny comes from my visit with the girls at West Academy. When I spoke with them, one of the girls attending the meeting asked if I thought there would be differences between the content they post and the content students in the East End post. The girl went on to reason that she asked about these differences because when she went to public school, she posted a lot more selfies, but once she started attending a private school, she felt like she had to post "stuff that has puns or is witty." Several other girls responded in agreement, noting a level of performance that goes into their Instagram posts strictly based on where they attend school. The girls' assessment of this geographic performativity reiterates how Black girls' digital, physical, and conceptual spaces overlap; the West Academy group described how changing physical school environments influenced their conceptualizations of how others perceive them, which, in turn, shaped the kinds of content they posted on social media. Additionally, this discussion shows how Black girls both internalize and try to fight against stereotypes about socioeconomic status because the implications that selfies are inferior to witty posts and that selfies are more acceptable content from Black girls attending public schools demonstrate how the girls have come to understand class. Ultimately, this part of the conversation revealed the everyday pressures that Black girls face to embody, perform, and present versions of girlhood that peers and adults in their various social circles deem appropriate.

Common Ground

Within each group of girls, their practices in digital spaces connected to the specificities of their physical spaces and conceptual development. Despite having different experiences with authority or peers at school, one event impacted the girls across age, race, and neighborhood: the 2016 presidential election. With the exception of the girls at West Academy, whom I talked to before the election, each group of Black girls that I conversed with brought up Donald Trump's presidency and its consequences at some point during our exchange.[36] We had reached the middle of the semester at Liberty Prep when the election happened, so I saw the girls in Digital Expressions the next day. A somber mood engulfed the building and felt especially heavy in my classroom. The usual preclass chatter had been replaced by a kind of silence people reserve for the saddest moments. Instead of pretending not to notice the energy, I took a moment to ask the girls if they wanted to talk about the election results. Destiny responded first: "I fell asleep, and I woke up and I Googled 'Who is the president?' and I just sat in my bed and started crying." Destiny's confession revealed that she started her morning in a state of despair. Kim chimed in to say that the results did not surprise her because "he was winning when [she] went to sleep." Both Destiny and Kim openly expressed their disappointment, but Jennifer completely detached from the conversation by talking about wanting to make a "Mannequin Challenge" video that she did with her classmates go viral. The "Mannequin Challenge" came about early in the social media challenge era and involved posing in place—like a mannequin—while Rae Sremmurd's "Black Beatles" played in the background. The fun of the challenge came from trying to stay completely still for the entire video clip—which usually lasted for the duration of the song's hook. After seeing many of these videos go viral, Jennifer thought it would be a positive form of recognition for their video to reach the same heights. Jennifer was the only person in the class of voting age at the time. Earlier in the semester, she expressed ambivalence about voting, and she never did tell us whether she voted in the 2016 election. From a point of speculation, I believe part of Jennifer's refusal to participate in the conversation had to do with the choices she made around voting (or not voting). Regardless of the reason(s) behind Jennifer's detachment, she clearly turned to the digital as an escape from the gravity of our discussion and what Trump's election might mean for her future. Conceptually, Jennifer wrestled with her own sense of responsibility around (not) voting. Whatever her internal struggles may have been, the disappointment of her classmates, who were not old enough to vote for themselves, likely intensified them. Since Jennifer did not want to face the lamentations of her classmates, and she could not physically leave the classroom or the school for the rest of the day, she escaped to the digital.

Jennifer's turn to a digital space in the immediate aftermath of the election may have served as a fleeting source of comfort, but most of the girls that I talked to had some level of conflict or anxiety-induced interactions in the wake of the 2016 election. For example, during one of the discussion groups, Sidney recalled a heated dispute she had with another student at her school who was mad about Sidney's political views regarding Trump. Recounting the incident, Sidney said: "So, I posted a picture of him and said, 'He's not my president' and put Trump in parentheses. And then this white girl commented. She was like—she left this long comment. She shouldn't have commented. That's my picture. Not hers. So, she's getting mad. She was the only one who commented about me not liking Trump. And then there was a whole argument because I have a picture with this white girl, and she hates Trump too. So, she was just pissed about it." Even though this conflict began in the digital space of

Instagram, the tension between Sidney and her classmate continued in their face-to-face interactions, and while the tension did not lead to physical confrontation, it did exacerbate the discomfort Sidney already felt because of her presence as a Black girl in a predominantly white environment.

Overall, the discussions I had with Black girls in Richmond, Virginia, demonstrate how they make sense of their worlds. Of course, the social issues represented in these discussions do not comprise an exhaustive list of the challenges Black girls face. Furthermore, the geographic specificities of Richmond cannot be applied uncritically to other locations. However, the conversations I had with Richmond girls do offer broader insight into how Black girls' digital content reflects the multilayered spatialities they encounter and navigate in their everyday lives.

"Loopholes of Retreat":
Digital Dissemblance and Digital Enclaves

Social ills, especially those driven by misogynoir, represent areas on Black girls' multidimensional maps that they wish to avoid. However, these realities cannot be avoided altogether, so Black girls must create means to maneuver within and around these danger zones. Drawing from and building upon Katherine McKittrick's theorization of the garret, I present digital garreting as one of many of BGA's space-making functions, which allows Black girls to seal themselves off from unavoidable danger, at least temporarily, within their multilayered worlds.[37] McKittrick uses Harriet Jacobs's story of hiding away in a garret in her grandmother's house, noting that Jacobs simultaneously "describes the garret as her 'loophole of retreat,' a hideaway," and a place of confinement.[38] Using this contradiction, McKittrick argues that "the garret can be conceptualized as usable paradoxical space" since it operates as a source of escape and possibility.[39] Black girls' digital garrets maintain the paradoxical nature theorized by McKittrick. On the one hand, Black girls carve out digital spaces for themselves in response and relation to restrictive physical spaces (i.e., institutions) and oppressive conceptualizations (i.e., misogynoir, classism, etc.). While these digital spaces are certainly not spaces of confinement in the same physical sense of Jacobs's garret, nor under the same social conditions, they are not spaces of complete freedom. As mentioned elsewhere in the text, Black girls' presence in digital spaces has the potential to make them hypervisible, which potentially increases their exposure to violence and surveillance. This holds true even when Black girls carefully create "private" spaces that should only be accessible to a select number of people that they choose. At the same time, despite these restrictions, digital garreting allows Black girls to exercise agency within spaces designed for their demise, and there are two particular manifestations of this practice that I wish to discuss here: digital dissemblance and digital enclaves.

According to youth media expert danah boyd, "The most creative teens often respond to the limitations they face by experimenting with more innovative approaches to achieving privacy in order to control the social situation."[40] For the Black girls included in this study, girls keenly aware of issues of surveillance, employing tactics of digital dissemblance functions as a way of mitigating hypersurveillance and controlling the situation. Digital dissemblance draws directly from Darlene Clark Hine's theory of cultural dissemblance, which describes how Black women "created the appearance of openness and disclosure but actually shielded the truth of their inner lives and selves from their oppressors."[41] My articulation of digital dissemblance refers to Black girls' methods of maintaining a private, personal sense of self even while participating in public digital spaces. Contrary to technophobic narratives that describe teen media users as naive and ignorant to how things they post may travel, the Black girls in this study expressed a sense of deliberation about their content, evidenced by what they post where. These girls "choose to share in order to be a part of the public, but how much they share is shaped by how public they want to be."[42] Across all the groups I worked with, girls said they post different kinds of content on Facebook (if they even have Facebook), Instagram, and Snapchat. For the most part, the girls who had Facebook saw it as a way to connect with their older family members (aunts, uncles, older cousins, etc.). Some girls said they would post pictures or updates on Facebook related to milestones (birthdays, graduations) or use Facebook to stay in the know about upcoming family gatherings. The girls who used Facebook described an awareness about language that might offend their elders and explained that they do not get too personal on Facebook. With Instagram and Snapchat, the main differences girls discussed between these two platforms involved the ephemeral nature of Snapchat; they liked how snaps "disappeared" after a certain point.[43] The girls noted posting more silly content or inside jokes on Snapchat because they saw this as a space where they could be more candid. In contrast to Snapchat, Instagram's archival nature forces the girls to be more selective about what they post as they do not want jokes or playful content to be misread by someone outside of their friends or peer groups.[44] One surveillance circumvention strategy that some girls discussed involved creating a "Finsta" or "fake Instagram." Even the name "Finsta" ties into its dissembling nature because despite being the so-called fake Instagram account, it is where girls claimed to post their most personal content. One girl explained how she posted videos wearing her bonnet on her Finsta because only her closest friends were allowed to see her in such an unpolished state. On the one hand, it seems like Black girls put themselves out there completely just by virtue of being on social media, but at the same time, the selectivity they exhibit in their content means we still do not necessarily know about their "inner lives" based on what they post on social media.[45] These tactics of digital dissemblance do not function to shield Black girls (or any social media user) from surveillance altogether, but they do show how Black girls attempt to control their environments.

Returning to the conceptualization of the garret as both "usable paradoxical space" and a "loophole of retreat," Black girls' digital dissemblance is a form of garreting. Black girls use digital dissemblance to maintain a sense of interiority, which they either keep to themselves entirely or only share with a small inner circle. In deploying digital dissemblance, the social media platforms where Black girls feel the most alignment between who they are and what they post function as potential garrets. For instance, among the girls who value impermanence as a catalyst of more authentic self-expression, Snapchat operates as a garret. Similarly, girls who want to present what they feel are more honest and fuller versions of themselves use Finstas as garrets. The sense of privacy generated from Black girls' digital dissemblance on and across these platforms allows them to utilize these spaces as loopholes of retreat from surveillance and judgment.

In addition to usable paradoxical space and loopholes of retreat, garrets are also defined by their function as a seal. In McKittrick's description of the garret (via Harriet Jacobs), the space kept Jacobs safe from the physical abuse of her enslavers. While digital dissemblance does mitigate surveillance on some level, digital enclaves help to seal Black girls off (temporarily) from the pervasive misogynoir they experience in their everyday lives. Digital enclaves provide supportive spaces that help Black girls cope with the consequences of violence and other forms of social discord. In her work on African American public spheres, Catherine R. Squires identifies enclaves as one response marginalized people have against their exclusion from dominant publics. According to Squires, these enclaves operate as (mostly) safe spaces and rely on hidden transcripts to maintain that safety.[46] Building on Squires's work, Catherine Knight Steele theorizes alternate publics in specifically digital spaces.[47] While Steele focuses primarily on blogging practices, her articulation of Black lifestyle and entertainment blogs as enclaved spaces has implications for social media as well. Both Squires and Steele emphasize the formation of enclaves as an assertion of (spatial) control in response and resistance to alienation. Since the girls at Liberty Prep had so little autonomy and safety in their school and neighborhood environments, they formed digital enclaves to create opportunities for self-expression and pleasure. Despite them being reluctant to talk about or show these spaces in class, the fact that the girls guarded their digital spaces so thoroughly speaks to the kind of affirmation those spaces provided; the girls did not want to risk infiltration of the few spaces they had to and for themselves. The Richmond-area girls outside of Liberty Prep also developed enclaves, but theirs seemed more driven by a need to combat isolation. The following conversation with Jasmine, a discussion group participant, demonstrates how Black girls attending predominantly white, independent schools turned to digital spaces to band together.

> JASMINE: On Snapchat it was like [a filter called] "young, Black, and proud." We [used the filter] with all the Black girls in my school. It's only three of us.
>
> ME: In your school or in your grade?
>
> JASMINE: In the upper school.[48] I'm the only Black girl in my grade. And then it's one Black girl that's a sophomore and one Black girl that's a senior, but she's leaving. . . . And it's two Black boys in my grade, but they re-classed, so technically they're in tenth grade, so I'm the only Black person in my grade.

While some of the girls formed digital enclaves with people they knew from school or their communities, others developed what Black feminist digital studies scholar Renina Jarmon describes as an online tribe by turning to social media to find like-minded people to counter the alienation that they may experience in their physical spaces.[49]

> ANYA: [Online] is the only place where I feel like I can go there and actually talk about stuff.
>
> ME: You mean like a place where you can just speak freely?
>
> ANYA: Yeah.
>
> TANIA: But you still get judged either way.
>
> ANYA: I don't care. That's like the only place I go to be myself. Like, I don't really talk that much in school. Out of school, but, like, when I'm posting stuff, then I will.

Tania's insistence that people still get judged online corresponds to the digital as an ambivalent space. However, Anya's response mirrors Harriet Jacobs's sentiment about the garret: yes, it was a space of confinement, but it also was a space for her to dream about freedom. For Anya, no, the digital did not provide a complete escape from judgment, but it did offer something better than the loneliness she experienced in school, where she admittedly had few friends. Even though the concept of digital enclaves as communities seems contradictory to Jacobs's solitude, both spaces still operate as garrets in their use as seals.

Ultimately, digital garreting illustrates Black girls' creative praxis. While neither digital dissemblance nor digital enclaves fully eradicates the risks of posting content online, these digital practices provide some sense of agential balance to situations where Black girls have little to no control. I do not present digital dissemblance and forming digital enclaves to suggest that these strategies are exclusive to Black girls; it would be intellectually dishonest to imply that Black girls are the only ones who have reason and the means to minimize surveillance and form online communities. However, Black girls' deployment of digital garreting is unique to their experiences of navigating Black girlhood within and against anti-Black-girl societies.

Conclusion: Creating Places to Be

(Re)invention lies at the heart of Black girl autopoetics (BGA). As a spatiotemporal technology, BGA allows Black girls to assess their surroundings and construct digital spaces of refuge based on how these digital spaces overlap with physical and conceptual spaces. Through their digital practices, the Richmond-area Black girls whose stories play out in this chapter enact spatiotemporal (re)invention on at least two levels. First, each group of girls used their lived experiences to create digital spaces that corresponded to their physical and conceptual spaces. Regardless of differences in physical environment and experience-informed worldviews, the girls at Liberty Prep, at West Academy, and in the discussion groups utilized social media applications to create digital space(s) conducive to an expansion of autonomy and communal support. Second, the girls' methods of mapping inspire both a reorientation to space as multidimensional and a reconstruction of how maps look and function. Usually, we think of maps as a coherent, two-dimensional visualization of space. For instance, a map of a country depicts all the states, provinces, and regions of that country on one surface. Similarly, a conceptual map might depict a writer's thought process on one sheet of paper or one collated set of papers. While Black girls' digital practices evince their multilayered worlds, their digital content does not reflect points plotted on one unified surface. Instead, their digital productions are disbursed across various platforms. Therefore, the way Black girls map their worlds through digital content does not adhere to any established or standardized method of map-making. In this sense, Black girls have created an alternate approach to cartography that adequately encapsulates the complexities of their spatial formations.

Even though the Richmond-area girls' spatialities were undoubtedly informed by their location, the connections between physical location, conceptual realities, and digital practices have broad implications for how we understand the digital as spatial, elucidating the complicated, overlapping geographies of digital, physical, and conceptual spaces. Geography as a field has started to acknowledge the digital as a legitimate geographic subject of analysis. Still, formal and informal conversations I continue to have with people—especially those not situated in the fields of geography or digital media studies—reflect a persistent bifurcation of digital space and physical space that positions the digital as abstract or "unreal."[50] Therefore, Black girls' digital practices help to concretize spaces that are often seen as abstract in ways that obscure their material value and impact.

While the digital is certainly not without (unspoken) rules and limitations, it provides Black girls with an outlet and opportunities for agency within contexts where so many challenges related to their schools, neighborhoods, and broader social environments seem beyond their control. As discussion group participant Tania put it: "In my opinion, I think it's better to be with technology because you don't really use paper and pen like that anymore. You use laptops, so why not just be able to go on technology when you need it instead of just when you're told?" Tania's insistence on a *need* to use technology beyond "when you're told" speaks to Black girls' multilayered social dynamics. The freedom to use digital tools beyond the scope of the classroom, which tends to be a space of restriction, allows Black girls to undermine the lack of authority they experience in a range of everyday interactions. Overall, the observations of and conversations with Black girls in Richmond, Virginia, speak to how Black girls' digital practices create and expand places where they can simply *be*.

"You Gotta Show Your Life"

2

Reading the Digital Archives of Everyday Black Girlhood

DESTINY: I was on Snapchat all weekend looking at friends' snaps.
ASHLEIGH (ME): Okay. Is that mostly when you use Snapchat, on the weekends?
DESTINY: No, I use Snapchat every day.
JENNIFER: Especially when you lit. You gotta show your life.

My love for stories and storytelling extends as far back as I can remember. Being an early reader growing up in the small town of Kinston, North Carolina, to parents who could not afford a lot of travel, stories became my outlet. Whether through reading or writing stories, getting lost in narrative gave me a way to explore life beyond our small town. My parents appreciated the fact that I loved to read (I often chose books over toys for my payday treat) so much that they never really paid attention to *what* I read. One day, as I accompanied my father on a rather mundane trip to the grocery store, I stood in line as he unloaded the groceries at the register, and a magazine caught my eye. I was captivated by the girl on the magazine cover. She had glowing skin and long, flowing, blondish hair. As the cashier finished ringing up my dad's items, I handed him the magazine and asked if he could buy it. Of course, he indulged; I handed him reading material, not a candy bar. How could he deny his story-loving child an opportunity to satisfy her insatiable craving to read? Delighted, I carried the magazine in my hands as we walked out the store. It was my first issue of *Seventeen*; I was nine years old.

Seventeen became a regular part of my reading throughout elementary school well into high school. We could not afford a subscription, so I bought copies whenever I had a few dollars to spare from the sporadic allowance I would get from either of my parents. I would catch up on the issues I could not purchase via the copies in the school libraries. In all those years reading *Seventeen*, I do not remember seeing any girls in the magazine who looked like me: dark-skinned, kinky hair, and "overdeveloped."[1] Unlike the media-literate adult I am now, I did not have the knowledge or analytical capacity to understand that the lack of representation of dark-skinned Black girls in mainstream magazines, and visual media more broadly, was a bigger systemic problem that meant nothing about my value as a Black girl. Instead, I concluded that the girls in those magazines were pretty, desired, and important. To use Lorraine O'Grady's term, I had been completely "unmirrored" by years of image consumption that both convinced me of my deviation from mainstream beauty ideals and taught me that the stories of Black girls like me did not matter.[2]

The conversation that opens this chapter resurfaced those memories of scouring the media I consumed as an adolescent for glimpses of dark skin and kinky hair. This exchange happened during my time volunteer teaching (i.e., conducting participant observation) at Liberty Prep in Richmond, Virginia.[3] At this point, during our Digital Expressions class four Black girls were talking about their weekends, which had become a common practice for helping us get into discussions on Mondays. The girls talked often about their activity on Snapchat, whether about content they shared or posts they had seen from others, but this was the first time any of them explicitly mentioned a specific motivation for using Snapchat. While Jennifer's insistence that "you gotta show your life" reflects a compulsion driven by any number of factors (visibility, recognition, performativity, commercial participation, etc.), her exclamation speaks to the ways in which Black girls use digital media to present, interpret, and respond to their multiple social worlds. Jennifer's claim in the opening dialogue reflects a sense of obligation that not only functions as an act of storytelling but also corresponds to the need for Black girls to represent, or better yet re-present, their lives within sociocultural contexts that actively contribute to their erasure.[4]

Although the image economy in the United States has become more inclusive (at least on a superficial level) since my days of consuming teen-targeted media in the 1990s and early 2000s, the lack of diverse representation of Black girlhood in mainstream media persists. When Black girls do appear in popular magazines, television shows, and films, their presence often amounts to tokenization or trauma porn.[5] Of course, Black girls who experience trauma deserve to see themselves reflected, but the myopic representational approach that reduces Black girls to their trauma actively erases other equally important experiences of Black girlhood. Given these realities, the visual field, particularly in its manifestation within mainstream media sources like (digital) magazines, television shows, and films, constitutes one battleground for the fight against Black girls' erasure.

While media erasure of Black girls might be seen as symbolic (though not insignificant), Black girls also face possibilities for material erasure. As illustrated by the struggles of the girls in Digital Expressions and other Richmond-area girls that I discuss in the first chapter, K-12 schools tend to be places where Black girls experience dissonance between who they understand themselves to be and how others, especially the adults responsible for their education, perceive them.[6] These warped perceptions of Black girls' attitudes and behaviors have a direct impact on how people in authority treat them. Starting as early as preschool, Black girls who attend public schools in the United States "are more likely to be suspended from school, more likely to suffer corporal punishment, and are more likely to be physically restrained."[7] Such disproportionate disciplinary actions not only silence Black girls within the school environment but also increase the chances that they will disappear into the school-to-prison pipeline, both of which function as erasure.[8] In addition to the violence Black girls experience within schools and the juvenile carceral system, "school-age Black girls experience a high incidence of interpersonal violence."[9] The disproportionate violence that Black girls experience—whether at the hands of their peers, law enforcement, relatives, or other adults in their lives—corresponds to a lack of support services and resources available to Black girls. Therefore, the societal impulse to devalue Black girls' overall well-being is another force that contributes to their erasure.

As a tool of creation and preservation, Black girl autopoetics (BGA) empowers Black girls to construct narratives of their everyday experiences against these forms of degradation and erasure. Black girls' digital content, especially on image-based platforms, often functions not only as evidence of their social interactions but also as a way for Black girls to show their lives. Vernacular image-making describes "a genre of everyday image-making most often created by amateur photographers and intended as documents of personal history."[10] This chapter provides an analysis of Black girls' vernacular images that reads them collectively as archives of Black girlhood. I show how Black girls use social media to document their lives and what they value in the processes of recording and telling their stories. The chapter places the types of events and milestones Black girls share online within broader traditions of Black American vernacular image-making to demonstrate the historic role of image-based documentation in maintaining Black memory. Through analysis of Black girls' everyday images, we come to see how Black girls use social media as a means of self-curation—a process that simultaneously involves thoughtful selection of images to share on social media and creates a sense of authority for Black girls regarding their image(s).[11] In these ways, Black girls' vernacular image-making forms an integral part of BGA. In a material sense, Black girls' vernacular images add to the archives of Black life. In a discursive sense, these images narrativize Black girls within and against sociopolitical contexts that insist their lives have no value. Ultimately, I argue that Black girls' digital practices allow them to construct informal archives that not only provide glimpses into everyday Black girlhood but are also essential to the fight against Black erasure as they preserve Black girls' images, stories, and memories.

Black Girls' Vernacular Image Archives

Recognizing the archival value of Black girls' digital media content will require wresting our definitions and conceptualizations of "the Archive" from the grips of essentialism and totalization. The Archive, with a capital A, has a totalizing effect, defined in very specific, narrow terms: the physical building (museum, university, house) or the digital collection, which usually still have some kind of affiliation to brick-and-mortar institutions. In this instance, the Archive serves as both a place and a collection of materials curated based on institutional objectives that oftentimes end up being driven by (a small group of) individuals. While the Archive has been essential to the work of historians, anthropologists, and others charged with making meaning from the past, we should expand our notion (and search) for archives beyond institutions that officially label themselves as such to one that judges archives by what they do.[12] At their core, archives share a common denominator: power. Of course, all archives are not equally powerful, nor do they struggle with power in the same ways. However, all archives reflect a manifestation of power relations.[13] For Black Americans, and people of the African diaspora more broadly, one source of potential power within the act of archiving rests in preserving records of the everyday against a dominant culture that for so long only kept records of Black people in the Americas in the form of receipts and bills of sale. For example, Black Americans' family Bibles often became personal archives of lineage that functioned to preserve history in the absence of official documentation of

Black life.[14] Maintaining these types of personal or familial archives has prevented complete erasure, thereby adding some, if only minimal, balance to the power discrepancies between Black communities and institutions that have failed to adequately document Black life.

Black Archival Practices

Throughout this chapter, my discussion of archives does not focus on defining or explaining what an archive *is*. Instead, because of the nature of BGA as a praxis of creation, I am more concerned with the functions and operations of archives—what archives do, what they create, and what they make possible. Using this approach, I look at three primary functions of archives in order to understand the (informal) archival qualities of Black girls' digital content. First, an archive functions as a repository. As a whole, the internet is inherently archival, serving as a container for seemingly infinite types of digital material. If the internet comprises one big archive, then we can think of social media platforms as specific collections within the larger corpus. The design of most popular social media sites makes users' content accessible to their friends and followers until the user deletes the content. This feature is especially prevalent in image-based applications like YouTube where users can create their own channels as a way of organizing content. Even applications like Snapchat, where the content seems to disappear after twenty-four hours, have a repository function since most internet content does not truly disappear. In addition to its function as a repository, an archive operates as a record. Whether an archive of texts, images, or objects, all of these items reflect and document the moment(s) of their creation. For instance, a photo album with vacation pictures can re-present the physical locations and time period of the images while simultaneously documenting specific activities such as visiting a museum or going to the beach. Inextricably linked to its recording function, an archive also operates as a trace. Here, I discuss trace both as a hint and as evidence. The material artifacts (texts, images, objects, etc.) within archives cannot show or tell everything about how people experienced the past, but they offer hints about and evidence of past moments or lives. Of course, archival traces do not allow for exact reconstructions of historical events, especially in the case of African diasporic peoples whose collective pasts have been disrupted by slavery, colonization, imperialism, and war. However, archival traces do undermine erasure by signaling to the past and ongoing existence of Black cultures.

Vernacular image-making, especially photography, has been a significant archival method for Black people as it has become an essential component of documentation and storytelling practices.[15] For Black Americans, photographs reflect simultaneous impetuses to preserve the records of Black life against a history of erasure and engage in processes of self-making. Photography experts Brian Wallis and Deborah Willis note: "Since at least 1839, when photography was first introduced in the United States, the lives of African Americans have been circumscribed—some would say defined—by visual representations."[16] Some of the earliest visual representations of Black Americans maligned Black people by presenting them as criminals (i.e., runaways and vagrants) and caricatures.[17] Photography became so central to Black American life in part because it provided such a sharp contrast to the "graphic imagery, in the form of lithographs or woodcuts," used "mostly to satirize or ridicule [Black Americans] in crude stereotypes that helped to validate the racism of white audiences."[18] Photography helped loosen racism's grip on Black imagery by providing a means through which Black Americans could engage in self-representation. That is not to say photography eradicated racist imagery altogether; however, it created a level of authority previously unavailable to Black Americans on a wide scale.

Along with using vernacular image-making as a means of self-fashioning, Black Americans have used photographs to record history. The centrality of vernacular photography to Black Americans has been shaped by a collective sense of loss and urgency around preservation. Within my own family, neither of my maternal grandparents knew their ancestry beyond their own grandparents, a lack of genealogical knowledge that reflects a common experience for African diasporic people whose families endured the transatlantic slave trade. In the absence of both textual documentation (birth and death certificates, marriage licenses, letters, etc.) and vernacular images, what remains of many Black Americans' family history often dies with the elders. Therefore, some of the main examples of Black vernacular photography—studio portraits, school pictures, and amateur photos of events like birthday parties and graduations—hold significance beyond capturing the milestones of individual people and families. These vernacular images, oftentimes compiled in photo albums or adorning the walls of Black American households, function as personal (i.e., unofficial or informal) archives of a family's history. While these traditional means of collecting and displaying vernacular images maintain their relevance within Black American culture(s), technological advancements have meant shifts in both everyday documentation and sharing practices. For instance, the invention and mass production of video cameras meant that people could capture an event in real time in addition to having photographs as a trace of the event. The digital age, especially with the popularity of social media, has allowed, encouraged, and compelled wider sharing of these vernacular images.

In the United States, smartphones are ubiquitous and relatively inexpensive as a whole, which means every smartphone owner has a camera at their disposal that can capture both still and moving images.[19] Not only do smartphone users have constant access to a camera, but image-driven social media applications make the process of uploading pictures and videos from the phone very easy. In fact, some platforms like Instagram and Snapchat are designed in such a way that users can only upload pictures and videos from their phones (instead of being able to upload from their computers also). With such tools at the ready, creating and sharing vernacular imagery is not only easier than it was in the predigital era, but it has also become an integral part of socializing for a large portion of the population in the United States (and other Western countries and cultures).

Given these conditions of vernacular image-making in digital contexts, in some ways, Black girls' social media posts look like those of many other t(w)eens regardless of identity categories. However, some of Black girls' day-to-day digital content about topics such as school and social gatherings can have what Tina Campt describes as an "enunciative dimension" that speaks to "the enormous cultural work they perform in creating a sense of self, community, and belonging for their subjects."[20] While this enunciative function itself is not exclusive to Black girls' images, their subjective positioning means that the cultural work their digital content does *is* specific to their lived experiences as Black girls. Additionally, while the significance of Black girls' everyday activities might be inferred or extrapolated, Black girls' direct engagements with issues of race and gender facilitate construction of theories and discourses of Black girlhood.[21] While we can look at individual Black girls' Instagram or YouTube accounts as their own personal archives, certain motifs appear within Black girls' posts that might point to more collective archives of everyday Black girlhood. In the sections that follow, I describe motifs or genres that emerge from the everyday archives of Black girls' image-making across demographic factors like age, social class, and geographic location. These genres fall into five main categories: selfies, friendship, prom, graduation, and birthday celebrations.

Me, Myself, and I: Black Girls' Selfies

The selfie comprises one of the most common types of content I encountered while perusing Black girls' digital content. Of course, Black girls do not hold a monopoly on posting selfies. In many ways, Black girls' selfies align with the quotidian nature of this image format, which has simply become part of what people see and do on the internet. However, "selfies function both as a practice of everyday life and as the object of politicizing discourses about how people ought to represent, document, and share their behaviors."[22] In other words, selfies have multiple purposes that oftentimes extend beyond seemingly superficial motives, especially when the subject of the selfie embodies one or more marginalized identity. For instance, #BlackoutDay illustrates how Black girls (and Black people in general) have celebrated their Blackness through sharing selfies in digital spaces. The origins of #BlackoutDay date back to March 6, 2015, when the first organized effort of the challenge went viral. Based on social media lore, one post by a Tumblr member named T'von Green sparked the call for Black social media users to flood their timelines with selfies and other images of Black people using the hashtag "Blackout" and/or "Blackout Day."[23] Now recognized in social media spaces (and some mainstream news sources) as one official creator of #BlackoutDay, Green hails the campaign as a "celebration of Black pride, beauty and personal achievements."[24]

The sociodiscursive implications of Black girls' participating in campaigns like #BlackoutDay lies in how producing and circulating these images provide opportunities for Black girls to see themselves in contrast to the dearth of Black imagery in mainstream corporate media producers like magazines, television, and film companies. Even when Black girls do appear in popular magazines, TV shows, and movies, they tend to fit a specific mold: light-skinned, curly (not kinky) hair, and thin.[25] As social media user Journey posted on Instagram: "Blackout Day is important to me because it is a reminder of possibility. When I look at the media, I mostly see white. I never thought that black girls could be beautiful until Lupita N'yong'o and Shonda Rhimes."[26] Journey's reflection not only speaks to the psychological impact of media erasure on Black girls but also how the inundation of affirmative Black imagery through campaigns like #BlackoutDay works to reverse this damage. While Journey's comment focuses on media representation specifically, other Black girls' assessments of #BlackoutDay show how lived experience compounds lack of media representation. Renee explained: "I live in a predominantly white community, and growing up I was told I was not beautiful because of my skin color by some kids. I started believing them and thought of myself as ugly, and I started to hate myself." Similarly, Brooklyn shared, "Some two years ago, I would've told you I am the ugliest, most vile creature walking the earth."[27] Both Renee and Brooklyn's stories demonstrate internalized hatred of dark skin resulting from the combination of media erasure and everyday interactions with peers and other members of their communities. They also both cited #BlackoutDay as a self-edifying force. Outlining why she appreciated the campaign, Brooklyn explained, "Through things like BlackOutDay and seeing other people that look

Plate 1. Friends laughing during the YouTube "Whisper Challenge."

All illustrations by Al Valentín.

Plate 2. Cherie dressed for prom.

Plate 3. Robin's COVID-era prom picture.

Plate 4. Prom attendee seated to show off fullness of her gown.

Plate 5. Friend group at prom with Photoshopped crown emojis.

Plate 6. DeeDee's valedictorian picture.

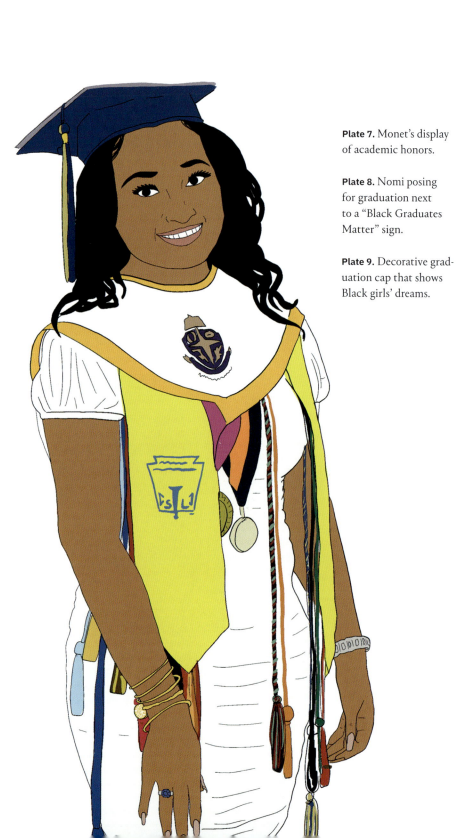

Plate 7. Monet's display of academic honors.

Plate 8. Nomi posing for graduation next to a "Black Graduates Matter" sign.

Plate 9. Decorative graduation cap that shows Black girls' dreams.

Plate 10. Another decorative graduation cap that shows Black girls' dreams.

Plate 11. Bella posing in the mirror with friend.

Plate 12. Briana with ratchet, fuchsia braids.

Plate 13. Archetypal ratchet pose: sassy.

Plate 14. Archetypal ratchet pose: middle fingers in the air.

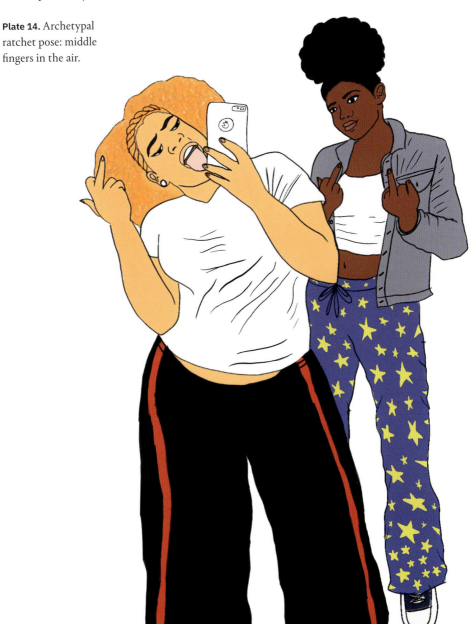

Plate 15. Archetypal ratchet pose: B-boy stance.

Plate 16. Lil' Kim pinup.

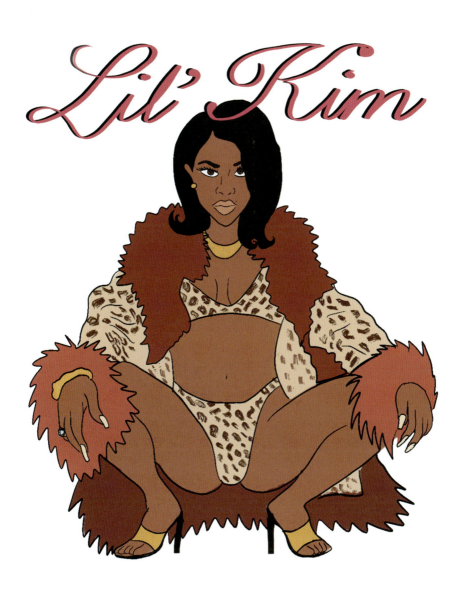

Plate 17. "Butt poking out" pose.

Plates 18–19. Tionna channeling Megan Thee Stallion in a "Hot Girl Summer" pose, no. 1 and no. 2.

Plate 20. Kiara's Nicki Minaj invocation.

like me loving themselves, I've come to terms with how I look and started valuing the things I have to offer internally and externally." Renee offers a similar reflection, noting, "Blackout day to me is very uplifting. It's telling black girls all over, [YOU'RE] BEAUTIFUL, [YOU'RE] FLAWLESS, LET YOUR MELANIN SHINE." These types of testimonies highlight the political potential of selfies for Black girls who struggle against being absented or unmirrored.

Even among Black girls who have not explicitly participated in organized challenges like #BlackoutDay, their selfies can catalyze connections with other Black girls. Within the genre of Black girls' selfies, natural hair images and references appeared frequently. More specifically, Black girls posted pictures and videos of their freshly washed hair, length checks (especially to show growth since the transition from relaxed hair to natural hair), and confidence-boosting natural hairstyles. Oftentimes, captions reflecting journeys to self-acceptance accompanied these natural hair images. For instance, Instagram user Janine used her posts on the site to chronicle her transition to natural hair. In one post she uses a split image of herself in three different poses with the caption: "At the end of the day, I ended up joining the afro clan." Responses to Janine's post included comments like "Ayyyee! Welcome to the clan lil momma" and "Yesss! Work it [Janine]."[28] Janine's post and her friends' encouragement simultaneously exemplify Black girls' self-representation and illustrate how Black girls connect around their images.

Black girls' natural hair selfies constitute more than vain statements of self-admiration or self-absorption; they oppose racist and colorist perspectives that position Black girls' unstraightened hair outside of mainstream beauty standards. The contemporary natural hair movement has roots in the "Black is beautiful" era of the 1960s and 1970s. A product of the Black Power movement, the mantra served as a rejection of and resistance to white supremacist beauty norms. The turn away from chemically processed hair marked one of the main features of "Black is beautiful." To members of the Black Power movement, chemically processed hair reflected a desire to approximate Eurocentric beauty standards. During this time, the afro became a political symbol that connoted one's allegiance to or at least affiliation with Black Power. While today's natural hair movement still reflects Black pride, the list of what counts as natural hair has become much more expansive. For instance, a person might straighten their hair with a flat iron, and that would still be considered natural since they did not use chemicals to straighten it. Despite its historical connections to Black Power, today's natural hair movement does not completely escape colorism or texturism. Even within representations of natural hair, curls are often preferred over kinks, evidenced by the popularity of edge control products, whose very name suggests natural hair still needs to be tamed. The girls and women more likely to have group 3 curl patterns are light-skinned.[29] Therefore, even within some natural hair spaces, girls and women with 4C hair who do not lay their edges have had to fight for recognition. The potential for colorism to creep into natural hair discourse runs counter to diverse portrayals of Black girlhood, but it does not strip Black girls of their representational agency altogether since they still have the ability to show their own lives through their digital content.

Black girls' selfies illustrate BGA on several levels. One, Black girls use their selfies to create spaces and opportunities to bond and build community. Two, Black girls' selfies help to create a discourse of beauty derived from their own experiences and perspectives in the face of dominant beauty ideals that would make them ashamed of their bodily characteristics. Finally, Black girls deploy their selfies toward creating a new source of affirmative Black girl imagery that did not exist (in such an expansive way) for Black girls growing up at the beginning of the digital age. In other words, Black girls of previous generations did not have these digital spaces to share images with each other. Yes, Black girls of certain eras had Black Power imagery, but Black girls' selfies in digital spaces reflect an agential ability—to create one's own images—that simply did not exist in the same ways before the digital era. Not only are Black girls providing more imagery of themselves and each other, but using hashtags like #Blackout Day, #MelaninMonday, #naturalhair, and #lovemynaturalhair makes it easier for Black girls to locate these images. Therefore, selfies allow Black girls to see and share images of other Black girls in potentially affirmative ways. Black girls posting their selfies on social media means that they do not have to experience the feeling of rarely ever seeing themselves within the media they consume. Communications scholars Theresa Senft and Nancy Baym caution against pathologizing the selfie as narcissistic, but even if we did lean toward such a characterization of the selfie, for Black girls to engage in what has typically been deemed narcissistic within a media culture that consistently denigrates Blackness and a society that restricts Black people's movement, the bombardment of Black selfies on social media reads as, at the very least, a disruptive act.[30]

"You and Me, Us Never Part": Archives of Friendship in Black Girls' Digital Content

The everyday experiences of Black girls can illustrate their confrontations with institutionalized oppression. One of the coping tools available to Black girls comes from the friendships they form. Despite the wide range of personalities among girls with whom I interacted on social media, friendships showed up in each girl's digital content at least occasionally, with some girls seeming to only post pictures or videos with friends. Whether these friendships developed at school, during extracurricular activities, or online, their centrality within Black girls' digital media production signals their importance for how Black girls both experience and navigate their social worlds.

Many of the pictures featuring girls with their friends take on a variation of the selfie, commonly referred to as an "ussie." In these types of pictures two or more girls stand together—sometimes posing in front of a mirror, making silly faces, and/or showing off new clothes—and take a picture that reflects their relationship. The content showcasing friendships is not limited to still photography, and a large number of Snapchat and YouTube videos feature friends playing together. In addition to playing on Snapchat and YouTube in general, challenges and tags also provide opportunities for Black girls to demonstrate different types of play. In online spaces, a challenge or a tag is a viral participatory activity where someone creates a dance, game, or set of questions and invites others to replicate the activity, sometimes tagging their friends and followers as a means of inviting or challenging them to participate. The "Whisper Challenge," for example, tests best friends' knowledge of each other by asking one girl to listen to music through headphones while trying to guess what her friend is saying.

In these types of videos, Black girls laugh with each other and show their silly sides (see plate 1). These displays of playfulness, particularly in the context of friendships, allow Black girls to contradict early adultification and undermine stereotypes about Black girls being mean and aggressive.[31] Early adultification describes a condition in which "Black girls are likened more to adults than to children and are treated as if they are willfully engaging in behavior typically expected of Black women. This [age] compression . . . renders Black girlhood interchangeable with Black womanhood."[32] The inability to see Black girls as children with innocence worthy of acknowledging and protecting makes Black girls more susceptible to violence and other forms of physical and psychological harm.[33] Given the material consequences of early adultification, these displays of playfulness serve as reminders of Black girls' childhood.

Alongside the images themselves that speak to the girls' closeness with their friends, their captions tell stories about the role that friendships play in their lives. Among the many Instagram photographs and videos of Black girls and their friends, love, longevity, and chosen kinship were consistent motifs. As one Birmingham, Alabama, girl captioned a collage: "This picture says so much about my relationship [with] my friends. All we do is laugh and goof around.... I love my girls and wouldn't trade my babes for nothing in the world." Her comment elucidates the importance of levity, loyalty, and love in Black girls' friendships. Another representative friendship image highlighting these motifs comes from a Miami-based girl. The picture shows two Black girls posing in their graduation regalia for senior portraits. They stand facing different directions while smiling and looking back at each other. According to the caption: "No one's friendship compares to ours! Daycare, elementary, middle, and high school with you and I wouldn't want this with anyone else. Thank you for being the bestest best friend ever." This picture speaks to the importance of lasting friendships and Black girls celebrating milestones together. In a final illustrative example of Black girl friendship motifs, two New York girls set up an event display together, smiling at each other as if one of them has just said something funny to the other. The caption reads: "We hang out. We help one another, we tell one another our worst fears and biggest secrets, and then just like real sisters, we listen and don't judge." For these girls, their friendship has become a kinship. The ways that all these girls describe their friendships in terms of sharing and standing together shows the supportive nature of these relationships.

Through these images of friendships, Black girls engage in creative praxis in several ways. Beyond the images themselves, Black girls create counternarratives about the nature of adolescent friendships among girls. One cliché about teenage girls positions them as catty, and stereotypes about Black girls having bad attitudes and being mean make this generalization even more reductive. By posting pictures of themselves with their friends, Black girls show that they *do* prioritize friendships, thus working against tendencies to pathologize teenage girls' relationships (or supposed inability to form relationships).

"Oh, You Fancy, Huh?": Black Girls at Prom

Black American vernacular image-making is as varied as any other cultural practice, but the documentation of special events, especially ones that require formal attire, reflects a set of broader conventions that shape both the content and staging of the special-occasion genre of Black photos and videos. Among the Black girls I followed on social media, prom pictures played a central role in their overall collections of images, and many of the images have similarities in style across years (time) and geographic location (space). Take Cherie, for example. In her individual prom picture, she sits in a chair underneath a gold wall decoration that matches her gold dress (see plate 2). She crosses her legs, slightly revealing her high-heeled sandals and fresh pedicure. Her dark brown skin shines as she places one hand in her lap with the other one cupped under her chin. Her look is serious and majestic. Cherie's prom image typifies a genre of Black girls' prom pictures in which they pose alone. In these images, the girls pose with serious looks on their faces, careful not to display a childish smile but instead to attract attention to flawless makeup with color palettes coordinating with their dresses. When the COVID-19 pandemic hit the United States right before the prom season of 2020, Black girls got even more creative with this traditional prom pose. One of the most captivating and resonant examples of this persistence in redefining the prom selfie in my study came from an Instagram user going by the name of Robin. In the series of images, Robin poses in an elegant baby-blue gown with a matching rhinestone-adorned mask (see plate 3). The series also includes a woman (presumably her mother or other female relative) placing a tiara on her head. The caption reads: "quarantine queen #prom2020." Robin's prom images exemplify how Black girls (and Black people in general) use setbacks and hardships as fuel for reinvention. In this case, instead of letting prom cancellations interfere with the milestone of prom, Robin upgraded the conventions of prom imagery to reflect the specific moment, and this type of context-capturing comprises one of the primary goals of vernacular image-making.

Another main goal of Black vernacular image-making involves expanding the story of the visual subject's humanity. Black girls' prom images do this work in several ways. First, Black girls' prom selfies show Black girls can be fancy and elegant. While it is important not to impose femininity onto Black girls, the feminine presentations within the images described here offer a potentially subversive contrast to how white supremacy excludes Black girls (and Black women) from the concept of femininity altogether, a conceptual foreclosure that has material consequences for how people treat Black girls. Certainly, not all Black girls desire to be feminine, but for those who do, their embodiment in these prom selfies contributes to a portrayal of Black girlhood that contradicts misogynoiristic relegation of Black girls to an inherently unfeminine category. Not only do Black girls' prom images show they can be formal or dainty, but they also show how Black girls have their own definitions of what elegance looks like. Slicking down baby hairs, picking out afro puffs, and posing on certain types of furniture (like the timeless wicker chair) all reflect Black girl beauty standards and aesthetics.[34]

A second way Black girls' prom images compel us to see their humanity is through displays of whimsy. Early adultification and disproportionate criminalization often drown out Black girls' propensity for whimsy. In prom images, we see Black girls' playful sides in their images with friends and behind-the-scenes videos (see plates 4 and 5). Black girls get caught up in the fairy-tale-like connotation of prom just like other teenagers, but people often associate the whimsical elements of Black girls playing with makeup and dressing up in fancy clothes as them being grown or adultlike. Even though the prom pictures I encountered during my research featured feminine-presenting Black girls, this whimsy also applies to masculine-presenting Black girls and nonbinary teens. In some ways, the idea of whimsy holds even more significance when thinking about masculine Black girls because it demonstrates a nontoxic form of masculinity.[35] Masculine Black girls need models for gender expression that do not force them to internalize and reproduce misogynoir. Finally, closely related to whimsy, prom pictures show Black girls' libidinal sides.[36] Recognizing Black girls' libidinal nature is especially significant for Black girls who come from working-class households, whose parents face criticism for spending what others might consider an excessive amount of money on prom. For these girls, prom challenges the idea that only people with material wealth deserve to have fun. Ultimately, Black girls' prom images encapsulate the (re)inventive qualities of BGA through displays of their creativity and through reorienting us to their humanity.

Pomp and Circumstance: Archives of Triumph

High school graduation marks an important milestone in United States culture as a whole, serving as an unofficial rite of passage from childhood to adulthood. For Black Americans, the importance of high school graduation cannot be separated from historical and ongoing struggles for educational equity.[37] While the United States has seen legislative and social gains in the realm of public primary and secondary education, underfunding of predominantly Black schools and forces like the school-to-prison pipeline demonstrate the persistent obstacles that Black Americans face in the pursuit of education. Therefore, as much as high school graduation forms part of the broader cultural fabric of the United States, its significance holds even more weight among Black Americans.

Graduation images oftentimes fall under the larger umbrella of selfies, but within Black girls' social media posts (and within the Black vernacular image-making tradition), they truly compose their own genre. Graduation photos have a specific grammar, especially in terms of staging. Along with these visual conventions, the grammar of graduation images posted on social media also governs discursive requirements around captioning the photos and videos documenting this milestone. For example, among the girls who graduated with academic honors, there are specific visual features. As a way of visually representing their academic achievements, these girls create regal affects by elongating their bodies, donning parts of their regalia, and wearing semiformal dresses, which are oftentimes white. Within Black American culture, the connotation of white dresses and white clothing—while rooted in respectability politics—often extends beyond a generic conflation of whiteness and purity. There is a sharpness and triumphant quality assigned to white clothing for celebratory occasions.[38] Instagram users DeeDee (plate 6) and Monet (plate 7) not only follow this unspoken protocol for staging achievement but also use the captions to corroborate the visual message. DeeDee writes: "She finished the race and she placed [first place medal emoji]. #4.4GPA #valedictorian [graduation cap emoji]." The staging of DeeDee's image combined with this caption shows how she distinguished herself by not only finishing high school but earning the title of valedictorian. Monet also signals to her accomplishments, captioning her image: "Freshman year I said I wanted my neck to be broke and I did exactly that! [star emoji] (not literally of course)." Monet's metaphorical broken neck refers to a desire to have so many honors that her neck would feel "heavy" from carrying multiple honor cords, a National Honor Society sash, and medals. Both of these girls use the grammar of graduation photos, specifically that of high achievement, to stage their triumphant images.

Another mood of graduation grammar still focuses on achievement, but this sense of accomplishment is one earned against all odds. Nomi's photo series of her graduation day includes an image of her squatting next to a car that has a poster taped to the back that reads: "BLACK GRADUATES MATTER" (see plate 8). The image speaks for itself, but Nomi's caption also highlights the photo's significance: "As the world spirals in chaos, I thank God for another day. WE DID IT, and it is now our time to become the LEADERS OF THE FUTURE. Stay safe. Fear is not a factor for us! #onelove #blacklivesmatter #classof2020." Judging by the year of Nomi's graduation, 2020, the "chaos" to which she refers reflects a tumultuous sociopolitical climate. In 2020, the COVID-19 global pandemic resulted in unprecedented changes in everyday activities such as stay-at-home orders, widespread school closings, transitioning to virtual workspaces, mass furloughs, increased unemployment, and business closings. The devastation of the pandemic coupled with an ineffective national response exacerbated ongoing issues like climate change and police brutality against communities of color and poor people. As a result, many children in the United States of Nomi's generation likely viewed this time period as the most precarious they had ever experienced. Given the heightened collective sense of anxiety in 2020, Nomi's image and caption intensify the sense of resilience and hope reflected in Black graduation images because her class still completed high school in spite of challenges well beyond their control.

Both the "accomplished student" and "against all odds" styles of graduation images fit into a broader narrative of this genre, which centers dreams. Several Black girls' graduation photos explicitly mention dreams in the captions, like Jade's assertion that "we really did it and we are one step closer to being everything we dream of being." Other images use visuality to present graduation as a realized dream or a milestone in a longer journey. Decorative graduation caps have become an expected part of graduation ceremonies in the United States. Sometimes, these decorations are simply that—for decoration. However, graduation cap decorations can also be an opportunity to make a statement. Both of these graduation caps speak directly or allude to dreams for the future (see plates 9 and 10). One reads: "Black Queen with a Big Dream" in the center with the words FAMU (an acronym for historically Black Florida A&M University) and "doctor" on the edges. This accomplished grad (Monet) positions her high school graduation as a point in her longer journey to become a doctor. The other cap pictured has a more general dream-oriented message: "Be the change you want to see in the world." The image is accompanied by a Bible verse from Proverbs 31:25: "She is clothed with strength and dignity, and she laughs without fear of the future." Both the cap and the caption intimate a dreamed-of future. Black girls centering their visions for the future in graduation images counters the ways discursive and physical violence often prevent their development and realization of dreams. The representation of graduation as an accomplishment or a milestone on the path to a bigger dream works as an act of resistance to those dream-crushing forces.

Not all high school graduates go on or aspire to attend college, but it is common for college-bound high school graduates to share information about their future plans along with their graduation pictures on social media. In the spring of 2020, the increased popularity of Michelle Obama's National Signing Day campaign coupled with the cancellations of graduations across the world due to the COVID-19 pandemic catalyzed a new viral genre of high school graduation videos: the college reveal.[39] The social media application TikTok launched before the pandemic, but the stay-at-home orders that ensued as a result skyrocketed the application's popularity. As indicated in the discussion of YouTube videos, challenges exist across social media platforms, and they usually make their way to all the popular applications. TikTok challenges usually center a specific song, and the participants do a dance or other performative act with the song as the script. For example, the viral "Don't Rush Challenge" videos included several people across different locations showing off different fashion styles.[40] Most of them started with an unpolished, just-got-out-of-bed look and then transitioned to at least two different styles of attire. Many of the college reveal videos started out as modifications of the #DontRushChallenge, where participants begin the video wearing their graduation gowns and/or paraphernalia from their high school. After the video cuts, they switch to wearing a sweatshirt or T-shirt bearing the name of the college they will attend. Another type of college reveal shows the graduate deliberating several options, choosing one at the end. This type of reveal shows that the person has several college acceptances from which to choose, which signals a level of accomplishment worthy of celebration in addition to graduation itself.

Given the role that high school graduation plays in Black American memories and family histories, documenting graduations has long been a priority in Black American vernacular image-making. Therefore, Black girls' graduation pictures online align with this broader history. In addition to highlighting a tradition, Black girls' graduation pictures function as a way of recording a specific moment or memory and connecting with family. However, one of the most important functions of Black girls' graduation photos in digital spaces—photos that can be shared and circulated well beyond the family photo album—lies in their testament to Black girls' ability to thrive in academic settings, against both hegemonic achievement-gap discourses and material forces that make school environments hostile to Black girls. Alongside graduation pictures and videos, several of the girls discussed in this chapter documented their experiences taking Advanced Placement classes, earning scholarships to attend college, and completing high school with honors and distinctions. And while valid critiques exist around limiting portrayals of "Black excellence" to educational attainment, the academic-related images presented by these girls demonstrate the wide range of Black girl personalities, interests, and talents that we do not often see in one-dimensional mainstream depictions of Black girlhood.[41]

This visual graduation grammar exemplifies BGA because it remixes traditional Black vernacular image conventions of graduation for a digital context. By definition, a remix retains elements of the original while creating something new. Black girls' graduation images maintain the regal, celebratory style of traditional Black graduation photos, but they also become part of a public archive that documents Black girls' achievements along with their refusal to be broken and erased by institutional misogynoir.

It's Lit! Archives of Black Joy

In the conversation that begins this chapter, Jennifer prefaces her call to "show your life" with an equally important clause: "especially when you lit." As a slang word, *lit* has a few different connotations, but the way Jennifer uses this word reflects its association with excitement. Being lit is an affective condition in and of itself and constitutes an example of Black joy. While lit expressions abound in Black girls' digital content, birthday celebrations appeared especially conducive to lit affects.

In alignment with historical Black visuality, Black girls' vernacular image-making includes both photography and videography. Several social media applications allow for the recording and posting of videos, but YouTube popularized making and posting videos in a social media context, solidifying its status as a platform for amateur videographers to share their work. One of the popular genres of video among YouTubers is the vlog. Vlogging is a portmanteau of "video" and "blogging." Black girls as young as toddlers (who have social media presences managed by adult guardians) up through high school and college use vlogs to talk about their everyday activities, give advice, and address the social issues they deem important. Vlogging also has celebrity potential—meaning that YouTube vlogs have been instrumental in paving the way to microcelebrity status for users who garner enough attention from subscribers and advertisers.

Within YouTube vlogging, there are subgenres of videos, and one of them is "Get Ready with Me," often abbreviated as GRWM or #GRWM. Like selfies, this subgenre of YouTube videos does not belong to Black girls exclusively. However, Black girls' GRWM videos contain cultural artifacts, expressions, and visual and discursive conventions informed by the specificities of Black girlhood. Alongside the first day of school and school dances, birthday parties are among the most common occasions that offer the backdrop to Black girls' GRWM videos. Even though "Sweet Sixteen" birthday parties have been a feature of United States culture for decades, the MTV show *My Super Sweet 16* might be seen as a muse for contemporary birthday vlogs. The show aired on MTV from 2005 to 2017, and one of its main characteristics was frivolity. Wealthy families spent tens of thousands of dollars on elaborate venues, expensive dresses, catering services, and oftentimes a new car. Some of the GRWM sweet sixteen videos do not differ drastically from the popular MTV show. Not only are the videos of professional quality, but the footage of the event shows Black girls dressed in gowns, fancy decorations in large reception halls, and huge wedding-style cakes. Such elaborate displays might seem like squander to some, but for Black girls, being showered with that level of attention undermines the ways that society routinely ignores them.

Even though some Black girls' sweet sixteen videos reflect an atypical level of financial wealth and comfort for the average American (especially Black Americans), other GRWM sweet sixteen videos reflect a more ordinary experience—such as having a birthday dinner or party with a small group of friends. The overall simplicity of these videos stands out as one of their key features, especially in comparison to the elaborate displays of wealth on *My Super Sweet 16*. The girls in these more quotidian videos celebrate with small groups of friends and family, but they still have fun. The simplicity of their celebrations holds significance because it demonstrates that Black girls' birthdays—and in turn their lives—are worth celebrating regardless of social status.

Within the vast archive of Black girls' sweet sixteen videos, there are a few common expressions and characteristics of being lit—across socioeconomic lines—that form a kind of lit aesthetic. Rap music, especially the trap genre, makes up one central component of this aesthetic. Trap music is a style of rap characterized by graphic lyrics and percussion cadences heavily influenced by Southern hip-hop.[42] Black girls who vlog on a regular basis typically have a musical introduction to each video that often becomes a theme song for the vlog. For example, YouTuber Naturally Golden uses Flo Milli's "Beef FloMix" as the intro for each of her videos. These theme songs might serve as an indication of the YouTuber's style or personality. However, the incorporation of trap music in sweet sixteen videos has a different affective purpose beyond identifying or characterizing the girl making the video. Sonically, trap music provides the soundtrack to lit expressions because of the upbeat drum patterns and heavy bass that make people dance. Visually, through imagery-laden lyrics, music videos, and artists' elaborate sartorial composition, trap music corresponds to being lit because its artists embody a celebratory spirit of living in the moment.

Closely tied to (t)rap, rapping or singing along with lyrics and dancing also signal a lit aesthetic within Black girls' birthday videos. Lit affect intensifies when Black girls engage in these actions with their friends. Missouri-based Imani's sweet sixteen birthday vlog exemplifies a lit aesthetic. Breaking from the wedding-reception-style parties that have come to define these celebrations, Imani had a small group of friends join her on a party bus (presumably rented by a parent or adult chaperone). In the footage from the party bus, Imani and her friends rap loudly to lyrics from popular songs of the time, starting with "On the Record" by Stunna Girl. During this part of the video, Imani and one of her friends mouth the lyrics while they dance enthusiastically. Then the video cuts to five girls yelling out the hook to Level's "I Bet U Won't," a song whose chorus presents a dare to listeners ("I bet you won't"), which inspires an embodied response—dancing—that accepts the rapper's challenge. By the time the girls get to Cardi B's "Get Up 10," they are screaming the lyrics to the song's opening. Imani's party bus video offers an apt illustration of how (t)rap music provides the soundtrack of Black girls' lit expressions during birthday celebrations.

Another fundamental sonic element of lit expression is laughter. Along with the kinds of dancing and rapping Black girls do in their birthday videos, laughter provides evidence of their enjoyment. Black girls' laughter, particularly in the context of birthday celebrations, goes beyond an expression of happiness to an act that demonstrates subversion in the following ways. One, birthday celebrations symbolize literal survival. For Black girls, to live one more year in a racist, (hetero)sexist society designed for their degradation and demise is radical. Black girls' laughter during their celebration of this survival serves as a way for them to laugh at their haters—*haters* here referring to people whose hatred of Black girls manifests as systemic oppression. Two, Black girls' laughter demonstrates their ability and desire to have fun despite all the forces that work to quell their expressions of joy. Ultimately, these birthday vlogs fall under the creative umbrella of BGA. Through their documentation of birthday celebrations, Black girls create Black joy itself and the spaces for Black joy to proliferate. Based on the frequency of these types of images within Black girls' digital content, expressions of Black joy are essential to lived Black girlhood.

Black Girls' Self-Curation: Troubling Notions of Authenticity

In contrast to image production as fine art, vernacular image-making focuses on the everyday. Historically, within Black American image-making traditions, "vernacular photographs are defined more by their destination than their origin. And, for the most part, they are personal photographs, bound more for the private album than the public exhibition."[43] In other words, part of what distinguishes images as vernacular has to do with how they function and where they end up. However, Black girls' photographic (and videographic) digital content explodes this strict distinction between the private album and the public exhibition. Traditionally, the public exhibition has been seen as the work of museums or the academy, but Black girls' digital content not only disrupts our understanding of the exhibition or archive, it also calls into question who gets to participate in the processes of curation and exhibition and to what ends.[44]

Self-curation describes a process by which we choose the details and information we will share about ourselves. My definition of self-curation builds on Cindy Cruz's concept of "storying the self" as integral to "the struggle against becoming absented."[45] My expansion of Cruz's storying of the self to self-curation attends to the organic nature of vernacular image-making (i.e., images that were not necessarily made as part of an ethnographic project) in digital spaces. Black girls' self-curation allows them to engage in self-fashioning or self-definition. Image-making provides an avenue for Black girls to resist mainstream erasure and distortion while asserting their own sense of themselves and the world.[46] While Black girls' self-imagery stems from their lived experiences in the present, like many other aspects of Black girls' digital practices, their self-curation also connects to a history of Black people striving to define themselves within and against white supremacist sociocultural contexts that render Blackness inhuman. For example, Black historical figures like Sojourner Truth and W. E. B. Du Bois understood how "photography offers individuals . . . a medium through which to create a vision of themselves that does not always square with how they are popularly perceived or with what we associate with those contexts in the present."[47] Both Truth and Du Bois used photography, particularly the self-portrait, to envision Black humanity and counter reductive caricatures and stereotypes. Alongside visual re-presentation, Black people have developed numerous linguistic, sonic, and sartorial conventions that speak to embodied meaning-making "outside of oppressive institutional structures and individual acts of violence."[48] These cultural practices demonstrate a tradition of how Black people have utilized visuality, and its subsequent discourses, as a means of self-definition. Ultimately, self-fashioning is an inventive, oftentimes innovative, mode of subjective expression, and Black girls' self-curation in digital spaces fits within this history of Black people deploying their own images to re-present their lives in ways that better reflect their experiences.[49]

Not only does Black girls' self-curation give them a sense of authority on a personal level, but it also speaks to a larger conversation about authenticity. Understanding "why a photograph was made involves understanding the social, cultural, and historical relationships figured in the image."[50] This contextualization allows for an engagement with and interpretation of Black girls' digital images that moves beyond or nuances questions of performance and staging to considerations of the conditions that produced those performative impetuses in the first place. In other words, the possibility of performativity within Black girls' vernacular image-making does not diminish the archival validity of their images. The digital self is not necessarily an "unreal/inauthentic" self but instead a presentation of a particular reality (or set of realities) toward a certain goal (or set of goals).[51] As an inherently selective process, self-curation requires fragmentation, meaning no one's digital self-presentation offers a full characterization or re-presentation of their subjectivity. However, those fragments form real parts of the subjective whole. And the realness of these fragments still holds true when self-curation is performative because the performance *still* becomes part of one's subjective composition and the digital (self) archive, broadly defined.

Overall, the power of Black girls' self-curation does not necessarily lie in their ability to refute stereotypes or prove Black girls' humanity because those are not Black girls' problems to solve anyway. Instead, the power of Black girls' self-curation lies in the authority it gives them to determine which images to share and with whom they want to share them. It gives them the ability to present the parts of themselves they choose to present. Creating this authority within and against disempowering social contexts speaks to one of many ways Black girls enact BGA through their digital content.

Conclusion: Rethinking Archives through Black Girlhood

Memory—both individual and collective—is a central component of Black American life. Related to the preservation of memory are the complementary processes of storytelling and archiving. While both oral and literary traditions compose a critical part of the Black American storytelling tradition, visuality also plays a key role in narrativizing Black life and preserving collective Black memory. The invention of photography marked a significant time in the evolution of the documentation and archiving of Black life, and the mass production of cameras allowed everyday Black Americans to document their experiences through photography. The camcorder enhanced memory-building even more through the ability to record things in real time. Both of these technologies have facilitated preservation of Black memory in a way that simply was not possible before their invention, and the photographic and videographic capabilities of cell phones have enhanced the image-based preservation of Black life and Black stories even more. While Black girls' digital documentation practices correspond to a history of Black vernacular photography, they also show us the importance of building and maintaining archives of the moment. As Jennifer Morgan writes: "The archive suggests itself as the place that houses the past, but in fact, its meaning is primarily that of the future."[52] Black girls' archival work (whether intentional or not) makes evident this relationship between the archive and time. Therefore, Black girls' creation of informal archives through their digital content attests to Black girl autopoetics as a spatiotemporal formation. Black girls' digital documentation practices allow for archival worlding, giving us both clues about the past and keys to the future.

Social media platforms, as corporate entities, have significant limitations regarding their durability as archives of Black memory because profit drives their functionalities and availability. While we should not place the responsibility of collecting Black memory exclusively in the hands of corporate actors, social media applications offer a readily accessible tool for Black girls to document their lives in this moment. Black girls' vernacular image-making and exhibition within these spaces offer important departure points for rethinking the relationship between Black memory, Black life, and Black survival. The way Black girls record their lives demonstrates how the preservation of memory is not a task solely for academics or trained professionals. Because Black girls' cultural work as informal digital archivists illustrates their desires to show their lives while simultaneously highlighting the precarity of where their archives exist currently, Black girls need *all of us* to be keepers of Black memory. Black girls show us that documenting the everyday will be a key part of preserving Black memory, and therefore Black life.

"I Love Posting Pictures of Myself!"   3
Hypervisibility as a Politics of Refusal

I love posting pictures of myself! I was never confident growing up and now that I genuinely love the way I look, I always want to show the world. I feel as though my beauty makes people uncomfortable, so I always post myself to make others who don't feel the mold of beauty feel more confident. —BELLA, 16

When I first decided to do ethnographic work to complement my readings and interpretations of Black girls' digital content, I spent quite a bit of time talking to school administrators and youth group leaders as part of the process to recruit Black girls to observe and interview. I wanted to have an opportunity to at least talk with Black girls about my work, and since educational spaces play such a central role in their lives, I knew I would need to go to these spaces to find Black girls. As a former secondary-school teacher, I also knew that I would need to explain my research and recruitment process to educational administrators. In my conversations with school personnel, almost all of them had in common a deep misunderstanding of the work I sought to do. Upon explaining to school administrators and other educational practitioners that I wanted to talk to Black girls about their social media engagement, most of them interpreted my role as one of policing: these educators thought my conversations with Black girls about their digital content would be an inroads for telling them what they should and should not post on social media. The initial enthusiasm for having me visit classrooms and summer programs quickly faded once faculty and administrators realized I was there to *learn from* Black girls, not to impose discipline.

One conversation stands out in my mind as both characteristic of how educational practitioners tended to view my research objectives and representative of attitudes about Black girls' digital media use more broadly. In an effort to set up a discussion group, I met with an educator, who I will call Kyle. Kyle, a white man, had extensive educational administration experience and seemed to have a good rapport with the students at the predominantly Black school he led. I met with Kyle to discuss the possibility of using the school he supervised as a site for discussion groups with girls. After I explained to him that I wanted to understand more about Black girls' online content, he said, "They're probably just posting selfies and sexting." My facial expressions tend to betray my attempts to keep my thoughts to myself, so I had to put forth extra effort to—as we say in African American Vernacular English (AAVE)—fix my face. I must have failed because Kyle went on to clarify that he did not think that teenagers, especially ones in middle school or early high school, had the maturity to post anything deep. There are at least two problems with his assumptions, both of which revolve around Kyle's positionality as a white man. First, it is racist to assume that Black teenagers have no depth. Second, it is misogynoiristic to characterize Black girls as hypersexual narcissists. Even if Black girls are "just posting selfies and sexting," reducing these acts to a form of shallow self-absorption instead of trying to contextualize these alleged behaviors flattens Black girlhood into a one-dimensional existence, a stance that undoubtedly influences (even if only subconsciously) how Kyle educates Black children, and especially Black girls.

At first glance, Bella's comments that open this chapter seem to confirm at least part of Kyle's suspicions. However, Bella's motivation for posting images of herself goes much deeper than the supposed vanity people like Kyle associate with selfies. I first encountered Bella's Instagram account in 2016 as I perused the website of a nonprofit organization devoted to the lives and well-being of Black girls. Each year, the organization offers a convention for Black girls designed to foster a spirit of self-love, education, and political engagement. As part of the promotional material for the convention, the organization profiles some of its accomplished participants. The featured girls share information about their lives, especially in relation to academic achievements, activism, and future goals, and several of them include links to their social media accounts. Bella had listed her publicly available Instagram account in her profile, so I began looking through her prolific curation of digital content, finding images ranging from selfies to excerpts of her theatrical performances to photos of activist organizing. Interested to learn more about the contexts and motivations behind Bella's posts, I sent her a direct message (or DM) via Instagram. The exchange that ensued was both fascinating and enlightening.

Bella and I wrote back and forth to each other about uses of social media. She shared details about her school, friends, family, and values with me. By the age of sixteen, Bella had a grasp of Black feminist theories that I did not develop until graduate school. Many of her Instagram posts highlighted the importance of intersectional approaches to feminism, and she prided herself as someone who understands the inextricability of her Blackness, gender, and sexuality. Bella found queer community in her friends at school, which was essential to her personal development since she had not yet come out to her mother. She also found solace in queer communities online, noting how she connected with "the conscious Black femme community" through her social media posts and exchanges.[1] Bella's assessment of the function of her different accounts speaks to her self-curation in different social media spaces. While Bella primarily used Twitter to curate her identity as an activist, her Instagram offered a more complex portrayal of her life as a Black girl. Of all the things Bella and I discussed as having an impact on her social media content, body image played an especially salient role in her online presentation. Even though Bella admitted to not being comfortable posting explicitly about fatphobia, her display of her own body (positivity) as a testament of self-love and confidence presented a challenge to the overall stigma placed on fat (Black girls') bodies. Instead of trying to shrink herself, Bella used her Instagram page to post hundreds of images of herself, oftentimes dressed up, having fun, and accompanied by witty captions (see plate 11). Because Bella's body size does not conform to hegemonic beauty standards, she makes herself hypervisible by posting hundreds of selfies online. In doing so, Bella flips the script about fat bodies—presenting them as lovable, desirable, and beautiful. As Bella indicated in the epigraph quotation, posting pictures of herself was part of a journey of self-acceptance despite the pervasiveness of externally imposed definitions about what it means to be a fat Black girl. Kyle's characterization of Black girls posting selfies and sexting as narcissistic and superficial contrasts Bella's motivations to post pictures of herself in order to declare value for fat Black girls. This discrepancy illustrates how the paradox of hyper(in)visibility manifests in everyday Black girlhood. The paradox of hyper(in)visibility refers to the conditions that make Black girls simultaneously hypervisible and hyperinvisible. Misogynoir provides fertile ground for this oxymoronic reality through rendering Black girlhood both excessive and devoid of value. On the one hand, the circulation of Black girls' images, whether by Black girls themselves or external actors, makes them hypervisible, especially within sociocultural contexts that require Black girls to draw as little attention to themselves as possible. On the other hand, while Black girls' images circulate, their subjective intricacies get lost in the reductive generalizations people make about them as a result of not truly seeing, hearing, or knowing them beyond their images, hence the hyperinvisibility side of the paradox.

Bella's Instagram offers one example of how Black girls negotiate and play with the (hyper)*visible* aspect of the paradox of hyper(in)visibility. As Bella's statement indicates, some Black girls embrace hypervisibility instead of shying away from its potential consequences. I argue that this deliberate act of making oneself hypervisible is a form of refusal through which Black girls reject the burden of externally imposed definitions of Black girlhood. These girls still have a sense of selectivity regarding their digital content, but making their public social media pages palatable to the gaze of onlookers does not drive their self-curation. Throughout this chapter, I identify three specific, though certainly not exhaustive, genres of hypervisibility in Black girls' online images: ratchet performativity, sexualization, and flexin. I present Black girls' acts of becoming hypervisible not only as a refusal of modesty and docility but also as a refusal to accept the designation of Black girls as the problem within an anti-Black image regime that renders them hyper(in)visible. In these ways, Black girls' use of hypervisibility becomes a tool of self-making or Black girl autopoetics (BGA).

Ratchet Performativity in Black Girls' Digital Content

Black girls' hypervisibility operates within a broader set of societal norms (and perceived deviations) regarding personal presentation and behavior: how we dress, talk, and inhabit space. During my time talking with Black girls about their social media content, I visited several schools and educational organizations. On one occasion, I visited a summer camp as a guest instructor for one of their daily enrichment activities. I opened the discussion by asking the girls how they understood the difference between girlhood and womanhood. One girl referenced the reality shows *Basketball Wives* and *Love & Hip Hop* to give an example of how women behave. The camp counselor in the room with us, Jessica, a Black woman in her twenties, dismissed the girl's contribution to the discussion, noting, "Those are not women."[2] Jessica further explained her position that the cast members of these shows do not conduct themselves like women (by her definition of proper womanhood); she described them as loud, ratchet, ghetto, and drama-filled. Jessica's assessment of the women on *Basketball Wives* and *Love & Hip Hop* demonstrates the unofficial, yet heavily enforced, rules that not only govern Black women's (and girls') behaviors but also connect their behaviors to their perceived level of (in)humanity. Black girls are always already hypervisible against a social backdrop that conflates humanity with the ability and willingness to uphold white supremacist standards of decorum, but some Black girls deliberately draw extra attention to themselves, especially through their digital content.

Of the visual social media platforms I examined in my research, Snapchat presented the most challenges in terms of observation and analysis. Unlike other image-based social media applications such as Instagram and YouTube, Snapchat does not have an explicitly archival function.[3] In other words, while we know that nothing truly disappears from the internet without expert manipulation, Snapchat's appeal, especially among teenagers and young adults, lies in its ephemerality. On Snapchat, the content users post becomes unavailable to their followers after twenty-four hours. In addition to this automatic disappearance, the application allows users to maintain a publicly available story that any of their followers can see while also sending personal video messages to individual users or groups of users. This means one could follow someone on Snapchat and still not have access to all the content they post. The disappearing nature of Snapchat stories and the lack of universal access made the process of capturing and categorizing images on this platform almost impossible. However, these same features made any motifs within Black girls' Snapchat content all the more noticeable, which is how the frequency of rowdy school cafeteria videos popped up on my radar. At any given time I decided to peruse Snapchat, I was likely to see a video of middle or high school students from various locations playing around in their school cafeterias. These lunchtime videos featured almost all the behaviors used to stereotype Black people and characterize Black students as unruly: loud talking and laughing, rapping along to explicit song lyrics, dancing (sometimes provocatively and on furniture), and generally being silly. These cafeteria chronicles often included a mix of genders, but the consequences of so-called unladylike behavior for Black girls intensify the instances of them being extra: extra loud, extra crude, extra ratchet.[4]

Ratchet, as a concept, has become central to Black American cultural commonplaces. While conceptions of ratchet are fluid,[5] in the most general sense, ratchet names a refusal to enact or uphold respectability.[6] The term *ratchet* connotes (sexual) impropriety, lack of decorum, and material and performative excess.[7] An example of ratchet material excess might be having long, artificial nails or hair weave that extends down to the waist (or further). An example of performative excess might be rolling one's neck while talking or making a popping noise between phrases or sentences. Like its linguistic predecessor *ghetto*, people often use ratchet as a pejorative, "linking Black bodies—often female and/or queer—with 'hood' or 'deviant' behavior."[8] As Jessica's comments about Black women on reality shows illustrates, Black people frequently use ratchet to disparage other Black people, especially toward the goal of maintaining class divisions. Given the association of ratchet with deviance along with the ways "ratchet acts...catch your attention and exceed the bounds of the acceptable," Black girls make themselves hypervisible by engaging in ratchet performativity, a phrase that I use to refer to a set of behaviors and bodily presentation.[9] Despite the attempts of racist, sexist, elitist societal structures to position ratchet as the incorrigible opposite of respectable, ratchet behavior and bodily presentation are imbued with agency and possibility.[10] Brittney Cooper's ratchet feminism and Michelle Meggs's ratchet womanism position ratchetness as a means to simultaneously navigate and trouble society's conflation of respectability and humanity.[11] Such theorizations offer fruitful frameworks for moving beyond a false dichotomy that renders ratchetness irredeemably inhuman. As a form of refusal, ratchet performativity resists oppressive norms and power structures that pit Black girls (and women) against each other based on their (non)compliance with respectability politics.[12] Therefore, in my articulation of ratchet performativity, I detach both the ratchet and its subsequent hypervisibility from their seemingly inherent negative connotations in order to reveal their affective and subjective functions.

Ratchet Style

Style plays a critical role in ratchet performativity, and hair forms a central component of Black girls' style. Hairstyles have become inextricably linked to Black girls' (and women's) subjectivities as they can make statements about identity and values.[13] Scholarship and popular media alike provide histories of Black hairstyling practices and evolution. From stories of Madame C. J. Walker's pomades and straightening comb to twenty-first-century legislation grappling with the acceptability of Black hairstyles for professional settings (e.g., the CROWN Act), the most robust accounts of Black hair evolution demonstrate how Black folks, especially women and girls, respond to racism through our hair, emphasizing a dichotomy between chemically processed, straightened hair and natural hair.[14] The dominant premise in these narratives suggests, in the context of white supremacist beauty norms, straightened hair attempts to approximate whiteness while natural hair represents a blatant refusal of Eurocentric beauty standards. During the civil rights and Black Power movements of the 1960s and 1970s, natural hair, especially the afro, came to represent Black pride and what today's generation of activists might call a *woke* aesthetic. Even though (natural) Black hairstyles can have a political function in responding to racism, discussions of Black beauty standards, independent of Eurocentric gaze or influence, tend to be sparse within the broad body of knowledge about Black hair. In other words, Black people have our *own* beauty standards that have meaning beyond reactionary jabs at white racism.

In outlining the complex, yet understudied, histories of Black American hairstyles, scholars of African cultures have made connections between the historical and traditional hairstyling practices and principles of African societies and Black American hairstyles.[15] For African groups like the Yoruba and the Mende, hair volume, not texture, was the true marker of beauty. For the Mende, "undesirable hair is *kpendengo*: hair that is 'stunted, not growing robustly.'"[16] This emphasis on abundance has traveled across time and space as Black American women and girls fret over people not seeing them or their female kin as bald-headed. In addition to having an abundance of hair, African cultures also valued styling hair, and this penchant for styling had nothing to do with a white gaze. Instead, among West Africans, proper grooming practices signaled personal, mental, and spiritual health while "hair that looks dirty and untidy" identifies "those who buckle under the strains of everyday life, retreating into madness."[17] These concerns stemmed from intragroup socialities, not a desire to approximate whiteness.

Like other forms of embodied expression, Black girls' hairstyles can send right and wrong messages within overarching cultural scripts that define what Black hair should look like and what it should do. Therefore, even within Black beauty standards, certain styles signal respectability while others are seen as ratchet. While the overall cultural messages and meanings of Black hairstyles continue to change over time, especially when it comes to wider acceptance of natural hair, certain styles remain tied to a ratchet aesthetic. Wigs, weaves, bundles, and other forms of hair extensions, which all appear in Black girls' digital images, have a propensity for ratchet interpretation. To be clear, hair extensions are not inherently ratchet within Black beauty standards, especially considering the connections between the hairstyling traditions of African cultures that utilized hair extensions and present-day diasporic hairstyles and techniques: "Both African and American hairstyles frequently exhibit a high degree of *artifice*. Indeed, where Western culture generally condemns most forms of body adornment or alteration as vain, deceitful, grotesque, tasteless, or at best merely frivolous, Africans tend to view *failure* to supplement, transform, or otherwise improve on nature as a lapse of character or a breach of decorum."[18] Not only does this analysis dispel the hair straightening as self-hatred hypothesis, but it also confirms color and extensions as part of Black beauty standards. So, if ornate presentation is part of a Black diasporic beauty standard, what makes certain kinds of adornment ratchet?

Within Black American cultural contexts, social class heavily mediates hair messages, and certain styles and techniques become attached to middle-class respectability while others signal "hood" status. Michelle Obama, for example, gets rave reviews from Black women about how her hair is laid despite the use of extensions to make it look fuller.[19] Similarly, actress Gabrielle Union has been very open about wearing weaves to achieve a polished look. Both women wear hair extensions that utilize real-looking hair and do not make them stand out in ways that attract negative attention. Both Obama's and Union's hair extensions align them with what Patricia Hill Collins describes as "the Black Lady" trope, which "refers to middle-class professional Black women who represent a modern version of the politics of respectability advanced by the club women."[20] Because women like Obama and Union embody the Black Lady, their use of hair extensions actually becomes part of their presentation of respectability. Even though we know these women's hairstyles contain some level of artifice, the realistic look makes them more professional and, thus, more indicative of middle- to upper-class standards. Hair extensions become ratchet, however, when they are extra: extra bright, extra fake (i.e., stacked styles and clearly synthetic hair), and extra long. Bright, bold, or loud hair colors such as green, blue, pink, purple, or any color that does not occur naturally are often considered ratchet within Black beauty standards.[21] Wigs and weaves that look fake and hair extensions that are too long—down to the waist, butt, or knees—or stacked high on the head also cross over into ratchet territory. Styles like Briana's long, fuchsia braids with interwoven white string that extend down past her waistline embody ratchet presentation (see plate 12). Briana's long, bright braids make her stand out among girls with more subtle hairstyles; they make her more visible. In this way, the braids represent excess in relation to social standards that demand Black girls eschew extra attention to overcompensate for the controlling images and external definitions imposed upon them.

Acting Ratchet

Along with the stylistic presentation represented by Black girls' hair, body language, such as the performance of sass, comprises another key element of ratchet performativity. Archetypal sassy Black girl poses and movements include neck rolling and standing with arms akimbo, the head tilted to one side (see plate 13). Black girls (and women) are often demonized and caricatured for having sass or attitude, but the sassy Black girls on social media invoke these very traits in an assertive manner that embraces the sassy trope, reclaiming it as a display of confidence, unapologetic self-assertion, and belonging. Black girls' performative sass refuses demureness and challenges misogynoiristic notions of how Black girls should behave in order to be valued and respected.

Other quintessential ratchet poses include rebellious ones like the B-boy stance and girls posing with their tongues sticking out while holding up their middle fingers (see plate 14). The "B-boy/B-girl stance," which came to characterize a hip-hop aesthetic in the late 1980s and early 1990s, is a unique way of taking up space, as the squatting gesture does not actually shrink one's presence but instead makes it more visible through contrast to other people in the space who are not posing.[22] Because of its association with male hip-hop artists and its spread-out nature, the B-boy stance contradicts ladylike presentation; it contrasts feminine etiquette that requires closed legs, crossed feet, and perfect posture. Therefore, this pose also operates as a form of gender-bending. Interestingly, a common occasion in which the Black girls I observed invoked the B-boy stance was in graduation pictures (see plate 15). By posing in such a manner for an event like graduation, Black girls create a visual paradox that both demonstrates their subjective complexities and undermines the false binary between scholastic achievement and the hood. Related to the B-boy stance, the "tongue out, middle finger(s) up" pose usually has flexible meaning. Sometimes, it can be playful, as in cases where Black girls strike this pose with their friends in front of bathroom mirrors. Other times, the pose can reflect a level of gravity meant to signal toughness or insurgency (as in the famous image of Beyoncé from the "Formation" video). Both the B-boy stance and middle finger poses embody ratchet sensibilities through their association with ghetto or crude behavior.

Overall, we can read these ratchet postures as rebellious because they transgress the bounds of appropriate or respectable (girlhood) femininity. Given the ways in which ratchet has become a concept frequently used to denigrate Black women and girls, Black girls' ratchet performativity functions as an active refusal of docility. When Black girls make themselves hypervisible through being ratchet, they subvert the restrictive behavioral expectations surrounding Black girlhood. Therefore, Black girls' ratchet performativity exemplifies the power of BGA to create, as Black girls' imagery illustrates, the agentive functions of being ratchet.

Hypersexuality as "Womanish" Agency

One of the main implications of Black girls' hypervisibility is how people read their bodies. The objectification and sexualization of Black girls' bodies works in tandem with their early adultification. Early adultification describes a phenomenon by which society sees Black girls (and Black children in general) as adults at an age that does not correspond to legal adulthood and occurs much earlier than their counterparts of other races. Early adultification coupled with existing stereotypes and controlling images that position Black female sexuality as always already excessive and insatiable means that Black girls' bodies become sexualized under a gaze informed by these distorted understandings of Black embodiment. Even when Black girls are not engaging in explicitly sexual behaviors or presentations, people read their bodies as (hyper)sexual. For example, referring to (pre)pubescent Black girls with large breasts or hips as "overdeveloped" suggests a flaw with these girls' bodies.[23] The term both positions thin (white) girls as the norm and marks all other bodies as deviant. Since the shape and growth of the body often cannot be controlled, people expect Black girls to minimize the attention their adult-like bodies attract. Therefore, when Black girls are deliberately sexual, their hypervisibility intensifies.

In her definition of womanism, Alice Walker explains how the term derives, in part, from the colloquial "womanish." Walker describes womanish as "the opposite of 'girlish,' i.e. frivolous, irresponsible, not serious."[24] Historically, Black women have used this term to describe Black girls they perceive as "too grown" and "fast," thereby making themselves available to sexual predation and exploitation. On the one hand, warnings against being womanish were meant to be protective given the sexual vulnerability of Black girls in sociocultural contexts that see them as adults too early and refuse to protect them. On the other hand, the accusation of being womanish and the general discomfort or unwillingness to engage in dialogue about Black girls' sexuality beyond victimization reflects a projection of Black women's legitimate fear and, oftentimes unspoken, trauma around sexual violence.

Dirty Dancing

Perceptions of Black girls' hypersexuality closely relate to ratchet performativity because both reflect an alleged transgression of good Black girlhood boundaries, and perceived sexual impropriety marks a defining characteristic of ratchet behavior and presentation. To illustrate how Black girls' sexual expression pushes them beyond the imaginary boundary of being a good girl, I turn to a popular-culture example. As mentioned in the previous chapter, the global COVID-19 pandemic gave rise to the image-based social media application TikTok. TikTok allows users to use music and other audio content to create their own one-minute videos. One popular video genre on TikTok, the challenge video, invites users to mimic choreographed dances, usually to chart-topping rap songs. The "Buss It" challenge emerged within this context and began trending among Black women and girls. Using the rapper Erica Banks's hit song of the same title ("Buss It") as the background, the challenge features women transforming from a relaxed, lounging-around-the-house look to a more polished, sexy look. But the main controversy around the "Buss It" challenge stems from the combination of participants' fashion choices with their explicitly sexual performances. In the laid-back part of the video, the user looks into the camera while a sample from Nelly's "Hot in Herre" plays in the background: "Checkin' your reflection and tellin' your best friend like, 'Girl, I think my butt gettin' big!'" This line sets up the transition to the sexy/sexual part of the video. The beat to Banks's song drops as she raps: "Buss it. Buss it. Is you fuckin?" As Banks's sexually explicit song plays in the background, the TikTok user drops it (meaning she bends her knees to position herself close to the ground) and twerks, moving her butt to the rhythm of the song. The dance itself is sexually provocative, but the user's clothing also typically accentuates the size and motion of the butt.

As the "Buss It" challenge became more popular, several celebrities decided to participate, including R&B singer Chloe Bailey. Chloe Bailey and her sister Halle rose to fame as teenagers doing cover songs on YouTube, which caught the eyes and ears of Beyoncé, who signed the duo to her label Parkwood Entertainment. People came to know them and think of them as cute, talented little girls and have tried to confine them to this characterization even as they have grown into adulthood. Bailey's participation in the "Buss It" challenge made it difficult, if not impossible, for anyone to hold on to an image of her as a little girl. Bailey started the video in a large black Versace bathrobe and a colorful bonnet: the kind that Black women and girls wear to bed at night and sometimes get chastised for wearing out in public. By the time the beat dropped, Bailey had changed into a black spaghetti-strap crop top with a matching skirt. The skirt itself was floor length, but the split on the camera-facing side made its way up to Bailey's upper thigh, meaning viewers could get a clear side view of her derriere as she bounced it to the beat of the song. Chloe Bailey proverbially broke the internet, going viral within hours and receiving close to one million likes on Instagram alone.[25]

While many expressed excitement at seeing the young star begin embracing her grown-woman identity, many others used it as an opportunity to slut-shame Bailey. Among the people who spewed vitriol at the artist, there was an overwhelming sentiment of shock and disappointment at her transition from a so-called wholesome, good girl to a seeming vixen. The critics and bullies suggested that Bailey should be more modest and that she was being sexual to get attention. But isn't part of the point of willful sexual expression to get attention? As the hateful comments continued to spread, Bailey took to Instagram Live to respond. In a tearful monologue, Bailey thanked her fans for their support and explained: "I'm just—Inside, I'm such a nerd, and like I'm not worldly at all. Like ask anyone who knows me, they think I'm like fifty years old in the head. But when I perform, and when I make music, and when I dance, that's when I get to tap into the sexier side of myself. That's when I find my confidence."[26] In the first minutes of the video, Bailey repeated, "I'm not gonna cry," as she wiped back tears. She became particularly emotional as she elaborated on her struggles with body image and insecurity: "And for so long I used to think I was like fat, and I used to hate my stretch marks and my cellulite. I'm not gonna cry [as she is crying]. But it's like now, I really love who I am, and I don't post what I post for validation from anybody or even male attention.... That's just how I find my confidence because it's taken a lot for me to appreciate myself and my body."[27] Bailey's comments about finding her confidence through dance mirrors Bella's motivations for posting selfies (described in the chapter's opening). In both instances the assertion of self-value comes not only from the performance or moment captured by the image but also through sharing that image in a public way. For both Bailey and Bella, image-making and image-sharing become a way to drown out the (internal and external) voices that tell them to hate their bodies. Throughout the video response, Bailey poured out her emotions, addressing the negative comments without directly repeating them while centering people who support her. Even though Bailey ended her commentary by assuring viewers (and herself) that she will not change who she is to fit others' desires and expectations, that she felt compelled to respond in such a deeply personal, vulnerable manner speaks to the deprecating nature of the backlash she received.

Although Bailey was a grown woman (twenty-two years old) when she participated in the "Buss It" challenge, I use her viral video as an example of a conceptual dissonance that occurs around the concept of Black girls' sexuality. On one hand, people project a form of arrested development onto Black girls who grow up in the public eye. This arrested development creates a representational fantasy in which Black girl child stars never grow up in the eyes of an adult audience.[28] By way of example, Black folks referred to former *Cosby Show* actress Keshia Knight Pulliam as "little Rudy" well into her thirties. The desire to imagine these Black girl figures in a perpetual childhood state reflects, at least in part, a desire to hold on to their perceived innocence. On the other hand, Black girls in our everyday lives have to contend with the psychological and material impacts of adults viewing them as fast, grown, and (sexually) deviant. People expect them to take accountability for their actions and expressions (and oftentimes the behaviors of others) in ways that do not apply to most adults (especially white men). Under these conditions, Black girls are unable to access the status of innocence that warrants protection. Accusations of Black girls being fast are rarely framed as a desire to protect Black girls' childhood. Instead, the "fast Black girl" trope paints sexually expressive Black girls as conniving temptresses who exploit the weak wills of adult men.

There is a cognitive gap between the projected arrested development of celebrity Black girls and the early adultification imposed on everyday Black girls. However, both the tendency to see celebrity Black girls as forever childlike and the characterization of sexually active Black teen girls as fast point to the same impulse: an obsession with controlling Black girls' sexuality and, by extension, their bodies. When Black girl celebrities grow up, the minute they engage in any kind of sexual presentation, it shocks the cultural imaginary, which cannot hold that perpetual childhood facade together with an explicitly sexual form of expression. This shock occurs because of a conceptual dissonance that cannot deem Black girls' *both* worthy of a level of protection reserved for childhood *and* sexually agentive. This conceptual dissonance has two primary consequences: it renders Black girls' sexual expression hypervisible and it creates a false dichotomy between so-called wholesome Black girlhood and sexual expression. Within dominant discourses about and perceptions of Black girls, sexual agency and Black girlhood are often rendered mutually exclusive in ways that simultaneously foreclose Black girls' healthy sexual development and absolves those who objectify and sexualize Black girls in predatory and denigrating ways.

For many Black girls, dancing is a connective activity whether that connection comes from the physical act of dancing together or from the "embodied conversation between [a Black girl] and [her/their] body."[29] The "Buss It" challenge represents a style of dancing online that emerged during a specific social and temporal context, but Black girls dancing in public is nothing new, and neither is conflating Black girls' dancing with sexual performance. This conflation means that Black girls' dancing automatically makes them hypervisible and hypersexualized under an external, misogynoiristic gaze that desires to discipline Black girls' bodies in general and with particular emphasis on controlling Black girls' sexual expression, desire, and performance. Therefore, when Black girls deliberately make themselves hypervisible through sexual(ized) expression, they surface the tension between external projections of misogynoir and self-objectification toward personal pleasure and expression.[30] External hypersexualization of Black girls reflects ugly histories and truths about their sexual vulnerabilities, but we cannot pretend adolescence is not a period of sexual development and exploration. Therefore, the desires of Black girls who want to invite sexual attention deserve a level of willful scholarly ambivalence that separates moral judgement from intellectual analysis in order to have an honest engagement with the complex realities of Black girls' sexualities.

Staging Sexuality

While Black girls dancing often involves (perceived) sexual movement, Black girls also enact performative sexualization by how they stage their images. Popular sexualized poses in Black girls' vernacular images include girls posing with their butts facing the camera, in a frontward squatting position with legs spread open (reminiscent of Lil' Kim's famous pinup pose, see plate 16), and sticking out their tongues while poking out their butts (either front-facing or to the side, see plate 17). In addition to the poses themselves, Black girls' clothing choices have a potentially sexual nature. To be clear, wearing short-shorts, miniskirts, rompers, and other items that fall into the scantily clad category does not automatically reflect sexual expression on the part of the person wearing these items. However, our heteropatriarchal society in the United States produces an image economy that imbues girls' clothing with sexual meaning in general and over-assigns sexuality to Black girls' bodies specifically. Therefore, Black girls deliberately showing skin, especially on certain areas of the body, reads as sexual, triggering colloquial phrases like "She needs to put on some clothes." This sexualization of Black girls' bodily comportment also shapes school dress codes and the disproportionate punishment leveled at Black girls around alleged dress code violations. Returning to the first chapter of this book, the girls at Liberty Prep who complained about the dress code noted how school personnel perceived their clothing choices as "too grown" (i.e., too sexual). The sartorial restrictions reflected in these types of sentiments along with how some girls' parents will not let them wear certain clothing items until they reach a certain age not only demonstrates how girls' clothing becomes sexualized but reiterates how people try to force mutual exclusivity between girlhood and sexual agency.

Finally, along with poses and style, Black girls invoking popular culture figures known for having sexual personas contribute to a form of self-objectification that refuses a simplistic understanding of Black girls' sexualities. Consider an image series from Instagram user Tionna, which features her wearing a T-shirt, short-shorts, and sunglasses and uses the caption "Issa Hot Girl Summer" (see plates 18 and 19). "Hot Girl Summer" alludes to a declaration by rapper Megan Thee Stallion, who claimed the summer of 2019 as one in which women (and girls) would prioritize their own (sexual) inhibitions over a commitment to pleasing others, especially in the context of monogamous relationships. Given Megan Thee Stallion's public persona and performative strengths along with her unapologetic sexual prowess and confidence, the phrase "Hot Girl Summer" has an inherently sexual connotation.[31] At first, Megan's sexualized branding might seem like just another bullet point in a long list of examples of how rap has become a music genre synonymous with the objectification of (Black) women. But closer reading of Megan's lyrics, interviews, and image production reveals her efforts to center her own sexual pleasure rather than that of men. In an op-ed for the *New York Times*, Megan shared: "I choose what I wear, not because I am trying to appeal to men, but because I am showing pride in my appearance, and a positive body image is central to who I am as a woman and a performer."[32] Megan's choices around her sexual expression reflect feminist commitments to bodily autonomy and self-love. Therefore, Tionna's use of "Hot Girl Summer" as a caption to accompany a series of photos—one which exposes the seat of her shorts while heavily accentuating her legs, and the other in which she squats in a position resembling Megan's twerk stance—has broader implications beyond communicating desirability. Tionna's decision to appropriate Megan Thee Stallion, whose sexuality has a clear feminist orientation, demonstrates the potential for nuance within Black girls' sexualized image play.

Kiara's Instagram pictures offer another example of how Black girls invoke the sexuality of female rappers in their images as a means of sexual expression and self-objectification. In one series of photos, Kiara wears a black crop top, tight black pants, pumps, and a small puffer jacket (see plate 20). Kiara uses a line from Nicki Minaj's "Hard White" to accompany a series of poses that are both ratchet and sexual (i.e., arms akimbo, butt poked out): "Trophy of the game, everybody tryna win me." This lyric in and of itself exemplifies self-objectification because of the trophy metaphor. Kiara's invocation of Nicki Minaj intensifies the sexual nature of the quotation and its accompanying image because "Minaj's sexualized performances utilize already available ideas of Black women's bodies, sexual prowess and promiscuity, and the spectacularity of Black butts and breasts."[33] Minaj's penchant for the spectacular coupled with her self-objectification creates avenues through which she engages in deliberate hypervisibility. Kiara's use of Minaj's lyrics summons the rapper's sexual affect, or what Aria Halliday refers to as Minaj's "anaconda feminism," which holds personal pleasure in tension with objectification.[34] Therefore, Kiara's deployment of Minaj as an affective proxy functions as an agential display of her own sexual desirability.

While these examples both rely on a kind of secondhand affective sexuality by alluding to famous women known for their sexual performativity, some Black girls present themselves in more explicitly sexual ways. Take Myesha's #quarantinebae image. The phrase "quarantine bae," which emerged during the COVID-19 pandemic, refers to a person with whom one enters a relationship for the sole purpose of having a partner while staying home to flatten the pandemic curve. In some ways, the desire for a quarantine bae reflects a general sense of not wanting to be alone. However, a brief perusal of the images associated with the hashtag makes clear the importance of sexual attraction among prospective quarantine baes. In her image, Myesha poses in the grass wearing a denim tube-top romper. She squats low to the ground with her legs agape and stares directly into the camera in a provocative way. Myesha engages in deliberate hypervisibility in several ways through this image. For one, she attaches a popular hashtag that will make the image easy to find. Additionally, the staging of the photo makes her body stand out against the monochromatic background of the grass. Finally, her clothing and posture accentuate the voluptuous shape of her body. Myesha's image illustrates a form of self-objectification that implies a level of both sexual desire and availability. By presenting herself this way, Myesha owns her sexuality and rejects the notion that she should not seek or invite sexual attention.

Overall, it is impossible to deny that hypersexualization poses an enormous challenge to Black girls and how they navigate their worlds. Hypersexualization has material impact on Black girls by simultaneously making them more susceptible to sexual violence and making it harder for them to report instances of sexual violence because authorities (and everyone else) will simply feel like they asked for it by being fast. Given the significantly detrimental impact hypersexualization has on Black girls, the adults who care about them—relatives, educators, community members—try to protect them by admonishing them about putting sexually provocative images online. Unfortunately, that protection oftentimes cannot be disentangled from moral judgment—even if subconscious or internalized. To say that Black girls are unaware of how people read their images is an infantilizing position that ignores how girls like Tionna, Kiara, and Myesha deploy sexual affectivity in their images. Suggesting Black girls modify their digital content to account for how others sexualize their images (1) assumes Black girls derive no pleasure from being sexual or sexually desirable, (2) absolves the adults who sexualize and prey on Black girls of accountability, and (3) strips Black girls of their sexual agency by denying it exists in the first place. To be clear, I am not suggesting that we abandon our warnings to Black girls about sexual predation and exploitation altogether; rather, I am asking that we do so in ways that help free Black girls from the notion that their sexual desires are the problem.[35] Black girls making themselves hypervisible through sexual images allows them to experiment with their sexual autonomy and notions of desire and desirability, which can be part of self-aware sexual development if we acknowledge the complexities of Black girls' sexualities. By forcing a reevaluation of sexual imagery, Black girls' womanish agency reflects BGA's tendency toward reinvention.

"On Instagram Straight Flexin": Black Girls' Displays of Pride

In addition to making themselves hypervisible through ratchet performativity and sexual imagery, Black girls also attract attention when they have qualities or skills in which they take pride. In the summer of 2017, then ten-year-old Kheris Rogers went viral as her older sister, Taylor Pollard, circulated images of Rogers at a fashion show. While Rogers's smooth, glowing dark skin garnered many compliments from social media commenters, her peers and teachers had not been so kind over the years as they tormented her with colorist jeers. In an interview with the *Undefeated*, Rogers recalled that as early as first grade, her classmates "would call [her] names and wouldn't play with [her]." She went on to explain an especially memorable and hurtful moment that unfortunately characterized her school experiences before the viral image, noting, "There was an instance when we had to draw ourselves, and my teacher gave me a black crayon instead of a brown one. I felt really uncomfortable."[36] To help combat the ongoing racial trauma, Rogers's family encouraged her to build a sense of confidence by continuously affirming her value. Along with her older sister, Rogers credits her grandmother with planting a seed of self-worth that resisted externally imposed definitions of dark skin: "My grandmother would always tell us to flex in our complexion. She put that in my head, and then I kept telling myself that."[37] Taking her grandmother's words to heart and leveraging the viral support from strangers, Rogers started her own clothing line: Flexin' in My Complexion, which has received support and promotion from celebrities like Lupita Nyong'o, Alicia Keys, and Taraji P. Henson. Since starting Flexin' in My Complexion, Rogers has presented the clothing line at New York Fashion Week, making history at the age of eleven as the youngest designer to debut at the prestigious fashion event. By 2021, Rogers had expanded her clothing line to include hoodies, rompers, and short sets along with the original signature-print tees, but her message remains the same: "I want to help others feel confident in their skin, knowing it is beautiful no matter how dark or light they are."[38] For Rogers, flexin her complexion was not only a display of confidence but a refusal to accept the racist, colorist projections onto dark skin.

Simply put, *flexin* means showing off. Rooted in hip-hop culture and lingo, flexin refers to a performative display of confidence that can be reflected in sartorial composition, body language, skills (such as dancing, playing sports, applying makeup, styling hair, etc.), or any combination of these.[39] For Black girls, flexin is an affective method through which they negotiate their hypervisibility by embracing its viral potential instead of fearing or shying away from its potential consequences. Flexin connotes a sense of braggadocio, thereby operating as a refusal of modesty. Although flexin describes a general sense of showing off, one specific form of flexin involves embodied expertise: highlighting specific skills or sets of skills. Within this genre of Black girls' social media posts, beauty tutorials and dance videos appear frequently.

Watching hundreds of Black girls' YouTube videos over a four-year span, it is hard not to notice the volume of makeup and hair tutorials in their content. For many Black girls who have curated their own YouTube channels, regardless of the overall theme or subject matter of the channel, at least one video in the collection offers an exploration of cosmetic products, oftentimes among the first videos to start the channel. This convention of trying to launch a YouTube channel through beauty tutorials corresponds with how cosmetics companies use YouTubers and other social media influencers to promote their products. Therefore, some Black girls have been able to use beauty tutorials as an inroads to monetizing their social media accounts. While this strategy seemed to have limited success (if any) among the majority of girls I encountered through social media, not all of the girls who showed off their cosmetology skills sought sponsorships or online influencer status. As Kari explained to me how she uses her different social media accounts, she noted:

> I can use [Snapchat and Facebook] along with Instagram to promote things I like and am good at.... On Snapchat I promote me doing hair. I like doing natural hairstyles, and I post on Snapchat so people can see my work.... I don't really have a foundation or anything like that for a cosmetology type of business for it, so I just keep it pretty informal for now by posting on Snapchat, at least until I figure out how to get out there and be serious about doing it as another hustle, ya know, have multiple sources of income.[40]

Kari's reflection on her skills and goals demonstrate the multiple ends to which she makes herself visible on social media. In addition to showing off her work,

Kari hopes to use any potential recognition she receives from posting cosmetology videos on social media to make money. In some ways, Kari's desire to have "another hustle" and "multiple sources of income" is not altogether different from those of social media influencers who review beauty products and post hair and makeup tutorials. At the same time, Kari continues to post videos of her work even without sponsorship. Unlike would-be influencers who abandon the beauty tutorial genre after sponsorship begins to feel elusive, Kari's hairstyling skills flex is more rooted in her present-day realities as she works to align her skills with a potentially more stable source of income that does not rely on the whims of corporate marketing strategies.

Another type of embodied expertise video that appears frequently in Black girls' digital content involves choreographed dance. These videos differ from the more informal dance videos described earlier in this chapter because they serve different purposes. Black girls' informal dance videos have an expressly social function—whether they are presented as a playful exchange between friends or an invitation for sexual attention. Black girls' choreographed videos have more of a professional function. Sixteen-year-old Paige's description of her dance profile on Instagram speaks to this difference:

> My dance page on [Instagram] is my "business" page. I use it as an online resume. People can see how dedicated I am to my craft, and that leads me to booking jobs, gigs, ambassadorships, and even a tiny fan base in the dance community. I started to only take pictures, and this "image" made some people think that I can only take cute pictures, and I couldn't really dance. So, I started to post dance videos of myself so that people know I am a very well-trained dancer aspiring to be amazing and that this isn't a game to me.[41]

Paige envisions her dance videos on Instagram as opportunities; they allow her to earn money and notoriety for her skills.[42] Her description of her dance page as an "online resume" demonstrates an intentionality behind the content she curates for her potential audience(s). Along with an entrepreneurial maturity, Paige's reflection on her Instagram account also illustrates the "I can show you better than I can tell you" attitude central to flexin, which tends to silence naysayers or, more colloquially, haters. By showing off her dance skills, Paige forces people to take her seriously. Even though Paige's dance skills allow her to create economic opportunity and respond to disaffirming attitudes, neither of those things operate as the principal motivation for Paige's flexin. Instead, she sees her dance content as a means of inspiration: "I want to inspire other dancers that have bodies like mine (because 'bigger' and 'stronger' body types are shamed upon). This is my life, and I want others to know that I'm not going to let anything or anyone stop me from being my best self." From this perspective, flexin does more than merely react to an external gaze. Instead, flexin becomes a form of intragroup communication among Black girls, telling them not to shrink or bow to others' expectations.

Both Kari and Paige demonstrate how Black girls use flexin to create opportunity. Certainly, there are serious, capitalist-inspired problems with Black girls having to make themselves (hyper)visible to generate potential income, and such a need takes away from Black girls' ability to simply be carefree children. At the same time, we cannot ignore the social realities that tempt Black girls to parlay their social media content into jobs. While we might wish that Black girls did not have to create their own pathways toward gainful employment, Black girls flip the script of their economic victimization by flexin. Even if these girls were just doing hair or dancing for the fun of it, which many of them do, that would be a subversive way of showing off because it dismisses the idea that all activity must be productive. However, the fact that girls like Kari and Paige can get paid to do hair and dance demonstrates the social value of their skills in ways that undermine society's attempts to devalue these skills as childish pastimes.

Black girls who make themselves hypervisible by flexin their skills or talents enact a refusal of devaluation. Understandably, some might push back against the problematic nature of Black girls (and social media users more broadly) using social media as a branding tool because it exacerbates capitalistic impulses to commodify any and everything. At the same time, in a society that values entrepreneurship, why can't Black girls flex their skills to create economic opportunities for themselves? Returning to Kheris Rogers, she used her clothing line to propel herself into stardom. While one could argue that being a celebrity diminishes her childhood, there are ways in which being a celebrity allows her to reclaim the childhood moments stolen from her in moments of racist bullying. The financial stability that she has created for herself also means that she can focus on doing childlike things (such as posting dance videos on Instagram) instead of worrying about how to get money to attend college (if she desires to do so) or take care of her family, which are burdens often placed on Black children sooner and much more frequently than their white counterparts. While Rogers's fame distinguishes her flex from everyday Black girls like Kari and Paige, all three of these girls refuse to let others diminish their confidence. They all utilize the creative forces of BGA to make the lives they want to live align with the things they love to do.

Conclusion: Working the Paradox

From the paradox of hyper(in)visibility derives a similar paradox of Black girls' visuality: on the one hand, Black girls use their images as a way to train us in how to see them. On the other hand, they refuse to take responsibility for how misogynoir corrupts our gaze. For some people, it is easy to celebrate highly visible Black girls who they perceive as assuaging dehumanizing caricatures of Black people. However, it is much harder for these same people to find humanity in Black girls who *are* ratchet, sexual, and immodest. Therefore, Black girls' act of making themselves hypervisible through behaviors and presentation that accentuate a refusal of respectability or docility exemplifies the creative force of Black girl autopoetics. For one, these images demonstrate how Black girls create agency in contexts meant to strip them of that agency. Furthermore, Black girls being ratchet, expressing their sexual desires, and flexin on people forces us to reevaluate the affective functions of excess and holds us accountable for how we see, treat, and value Black girls.

As a closing thought, I return briefly to Bella, who posted an image of Audre Lorde on Instagram in celebration of Women's History Month. I want to focus on two features of the post that speak to hypervisibility as a politics of refusal. The first is a quote from Audre Lorde, which serves as an introduction to Bella's analysis of Lorde's life: "If I didn't define myself for myself, I would be crunched into other people's fantasies for me and eaten alive."[43] Here, Lorde's words highlight the role of self-definition in valuing oneself and apply directly to Black girls who refuse to take on the baggage of misogynoir in their creation of digital content. The second aspect of Bella's post about Audre Lorde that deserves attention here comes from her reflection on Lorde's words and life: "To be a black queer woman is already a struggle in itself. But she took her struggle and she voiced it like no other. She was loud and demanding and she commanded space." In a world that saw Lorde's Black, queer identity as menacing, she made herself hypervisible by being loud and commanding space. While the girls I have discussed in this chapter may not have all read Audre Lorde, they have certainly followed her lead in terms of taking up space and creating a sense of urgency around their own self-expression, thus highlighting the inherent spatiotemporality of BGA. All of these girls demonstrate how deliberate hypervisibility can function as both a politics of refusal and an affirming methodology for helping Black girls (re)define themselves.

Making Time

4

*Black Girls' Digital Activism
as Temporal Reclamation*

Many adults of my generation have fond memories of their early years of school. Before the days of spending hours on homework or cramming for tests, there were the myriad discoveries of elementary school, especially kindergarten. I, however, do not look back at kindergarten with sentimentality; in fact, I hated it. Before I started school, I remember pleading with my mom to let me skip kindergarten. For one, I wanted to be in the same grade as my middle brother since people used to think we were twins back then anyway. More importantly, I felt kindergarten would be a waste of time because I already knew how to read. To me, learning letters, numbers, and colors would take time away from learning new words through reading new books. I am not sure how or why I had such a strong sense of (wasted) time at such an early age, but my temporal argument did not convince my mother. To my dismay, she enrolled me in kindergarten at the only elementary school in our district.

The first few months as a kindergartner went by relatively smoothly because I learned how to steal time. During nap time, while my classmates drifted off to sleep, I wandered in the worlds of books. At first, I tried to sneak to read, but my teacher, Mrs. Grindell, was somewhat intrigued. Upon learning that I could read (well above grade level), Mrs. Grindell offered to find me books, and most days, I would read to her during nap time. Unfortunately, Mrs. Grindell's fascination with my precociousness eventually turned into annoyance. She saw me as creating extra work for her even though I never *asked* her to find books for me since I was perfectly capable of finding my own books in the library.[1] Mrs. Grindell's irritation with me culminated in a moment when she silenced me and stopped allowing me to read during nap time altogether. During a phonics lesson, she began teaching us how to sound out words, but her methods were a little off, to put it nicely. She asked the class to sound out the word "boat." Then she spelled it "B-O-T." I raised my hand.

ME: That's not how you spell boat. That's bot.

MRS. GRINDELL: Well, I'm just trying to teach you to spell the words like they sound for now.

I conceded for a second, thinking that she would pick another word that is actually spelled like it sounds.

MRS. GRINDELL: Coat. C-O-T.

ME: That's cot.

MRS. GRINDELL: Will you be quiet?! I'm trying to teach the class how to sound out words!

ME: But that's not how those words are spelled! And when we get to first grade, they are gonna have to relearn how to spell those words, and they will be confused.

I remember the urgency in my voice, and it may have come across as yelling or being dramatic. Looking back on the moment, especially as a former K–12 teacher, I do understand how frustrating it can be when students interrupt instruction. But truthfully, Mrs. Grindell needed to be interrupted. Of course, I did not understand the concept of advocacy as a five-year-old, but I did have a sense of right and wrong, fair and unfair. Though I could not quite articulate my concerns in terms of a teacher's ethical responsibility, I knew it was unfair to teach children, especially children who looked like me, the wrong thing. Again, I was concerned with time—the time it would take my classmates, my friends, to unlearn the wrong spelling, which would in turn affect the time it would take them to learn how to read.

In front of the entire class, Mrs. Grindell yelled, "You think you're special just because you can read! You need to be quiet for the rest of the day. And you can't read during nap time today." I followed her instructions and kept quiet. I did not think that reading made someone special. In fact, I thought reading should be an ordinary part of life, which is why I so desperately wanted my classmates to learn how to do it. But the humiliation of that moment quelled my little revolutionary spirit. I retreated into my kindergarten brain and continued to wish my mother would have let me skip. It would be years later before I found the nerve to steal (back) time from oppressive institutions and institutional practices.

Part of how Black girl autopoetics functions is through reframing concepts that we already know and understand. As a child, I did not recognize the cultural ramifications of my urgency around wasted time or my temporal reclamation methods, but temporality has a long-established centrality to Black life, especially in diasporic contexts, which, by definition, involve spatiotemporal disruption and dispersal. BGA equips Black girls with tools to undermine the temporal structures of white supremacist heteropatriarchy. Black girls reclaim, make, and keep time in service of acknowledging the past, building in the present, and gesturing toward the future. Here, I do not discuss the future as a deferential elsewhere that becomes a container for all the problems we cannot solve or have given up on trying to solve in the present. Instead, I talk about the future within a specifically Black temporal context that weaves together past, present, and future in a cyclical fashion.[2] Therefore, I argue, Black girls deploy BGA to (re)create, (re)appropriate, and (re)structure temporality in ways that counter how time has been used against Black people.

My attempts at temporal control by reading during nap time started out as an individual endeavor, but I vocalized my concerns about temporality when I felt my peers' collective futures were at stake. I only had my tiny kindergarten voice to advocate for my classmates, but contemporary digital tools, especially social media, equip Black girls with multiple means of (temporal) advocacy and solidarity. To expound upon the relationship between BGA, time, and Black girls' digital practices, I focus on three examples of advocacy via online activism: Black Lives Matter in All Capacities' #FreeGrace demonstration, Marley Dias's #1000BlackGirlBooks campaign, and the Art Hoe Collective. I highlight Black girls' digital activism because it (1) features prominently in Black girls' everyday digital content and practices, (2) elucidates the key features of Black temporalities, and (3) enumerates the functions of BGA as a temporal intervention. Along with these general features of Black girls' digital activism, I concentrate on these specific efforts because they center Black girls in their digital content, and they demonstrate how Black girls fight back against institutions that rob them of their time. Of course, in an ideal world, Black girls would lead carefree lives that did not require their resistance against temporal dispossession. But within the world we have now, these cases show how Black girls can leverage BGA as temporal agency toward their own survival as well as that of their communities, thereby shedding new light on the relationship between Blackness and time.

What Makes Time Black?

On July 27, 2017, the United States Congress House Financial Services Committee held a hearing as part of its investigation of then president Donald Trump's financial ties to Russia. During this hearing, Congressmember Maxine Waters, affectionately known as "Auntie Maxine" among younger-generation Black Americans, took Treasury Secretary Steven Mnuchin to task about the Trump administration's potential collusion with Russia. Typical of such proceedings, Mnuchin danced around the questions and tried to outtalk Waters well beyond his turn to speak. Of course, Auntie Maxine was not having that. The exchange between Waters and Mnuchin went viral because of one three-word phrase she repeated throughout: "Reclaiming my time!"[3] Each time Mnuchin ignored the dialogical conventions of the hearing, Waters reclaimed her time, refusing to be silenced by Mnuchin's insistence on breaking the rules. Waters's declaration became a rallying cry for people who could identify all too well with having their time stolen, wasted, or interrupted. Black Americans, and African diasporic peoples more broadly, have a fraught relationship with time largely because of the temporal disruption represented by the transatlantic slave trade. From the trafficking of human beings, to the centuries of enslavement and colonization, to present-day lingering effects of these injustices, Black people have been robbed of time.

The aforementioned examples of temporal dispossession represent one aspect of Black people's relationship to time, but Black temporalities might also be defined by a tendency to operate outside of hegemonic colonial and Western parameters: "Blackness 'disorders' temporality through its refusal to be contained and constricted within dominant Western ontologies."[4] Take the Black American colloquialism "CP (colored people's) time," which can be meant as a joke or pejorative depending on the speaker and context.[5] CP time usually refers to tardiness, on the part of Black people, that delays the commencement of an event and/or results in missing important parts of an event. The notion of CP time features so prominently in Black American culture that informal invitations to events often include the caveat: "We're starting on time, not CP time."[6] In addition to these kinds of blanket warnings, CP time can sometimes inform how Black people approach individual interactions. For instance, if Thanksgiving dinner starts at 4:00 p.m., and cousin Sharon tends to run about an hour behind schedule, the host will likely tell Sharon the dinner starts at 3:00 p.m. to ensure she will be there in time to say grace and eat before the food gets cold. While one must be careful not to essentialize or pathologize Black people as inherently tardy, the notion of CP time does signal to distinctly Black temporalities. But CP time is not just about being late. CP time offers a means for Black people to exert control over temporal structures designed to disempower them. Tardiness comprises only one aspect of CP time, but it's not the defining feature; rather, CP time reflects the broader historical, social, and cultural contexts that shape Black temporalities. In other words, how we value, understand, and use time depends on sociocultural conditioning. Black people descended from cultures that prioritize social relationships over punctuality, for example, might conceptualize time in ways that position their own tardiness as a minor inconvenience compared to missing an opportunity to spend a few extra minutes catching up with a friend or listening to an elder's story. Paying attention to these nuances of CP time allows us to (re)evaluate dominant temporal structures as they relate to Blackness.

Throughout this chapter, my discussion of Black girls' digital activism as a conduit of BGA operates under two theoretical premises of Black time. First, Black temporalities are nonlinear. Bonnie J. Barthold's *Black Time: The Fiction of Africa, the Caribbean, and the United States* remains foundational to understanding Black people's relationship to time. In this volume, Barthold presents the primary distinguishing feature of Black time as its mythic, cyclical nature. Rooted in ancient West African cosmologies, Barthold's conception of Black time places the past, present, and future in a loop that repeats over and over. This depiction of time as an ongoing cycle between past, present, and future opposes a Western/colonial model that charts time as a linear progression to a future that is unseen yet seemingly conquerable with the right technological advancements. The West African concept *sankofa* epitomizes both the antihegemonic and cyclical natures of Black temporalities. Sankofa comes from the Akan people of Ghana and "can be broken down into three syllables—'san' (return), 'ko' (go), and 'fa' (take)—that can be translated into 'go back and take it.'"[7] When translated literally, sankofa means "it is not taboo to go back and fetch what you forgot."[8] The idea of going back is antithetical to linear progress. Instead of letting go of the past, sankofa encourages a return—not for the sake of living in the past but rather to connect the past to the present and the future. Scholars of Black cultural studies have continued to build upon the notion of Black temporalities, specifically sankofa, as a perpetual inextricability between past, present, and future. For instance, Kinitra Brooks, Alexis McGee, and Stephanie Schoellman developed "speculative sankofarration" to demonstrate the cyclical nature of time in Afrofuturist literary texts. Despite its name, Afrofuturism maintains "a central notion... that the Western construction of time as linear is a fallacy."[9] Brooks and her coauthors build on this foundational assumption along with John Jennings's "sankofarration," which he defined as a "conflation of Sankofa and narration, a cosmological episteme that centers the act of claiming the future as well as the past."[10] Sankofarration involves more than acknowledgment of or reflection on the past; one who engages in sankofarration brings back something from the past into the present and (possibly) the future. Therefore, each of these theorizations of sankofarration operate from the premise of temporal fluidity between past, present, and future.

The cyclical nature of Black temporalities tracks with physical scientific descriptions of time. From a scientific standpoint, Black feminist physicist Chanda Prescod-Weinstein explains the inextricability of space and time, or spacetime. Not only are space and time connected, but spacetime is curved, not linear. Prescod-Weinstein notes: "Spacetime isn't a room that sits in the background. It is a room that is interacting with its contents. The contents can only move around the room according to its shape... spacetime tells matter how to move, and matter tells spacetime how to curve."[11] While this relationship between space, time, and matter is not exclusive to Black people, Black temporalities reflect the distinct ways Blackness curves spacetime, a notion that leads to the second theoretical premise of this chapter: Black time is agential.

Along with nonlinearity, Black temporalities reflect agency. While it may be tempting to take a nihilistic approach to the relationship between race, especially Blackness, and time, the discrepancies between Black time and what sociologist Rahsaan Mahadeo terms white time represent a liminal space imbued with possibility.[12] Acts of reclamation speak to the agency of Black temporalities. As demonstrated by both Auntie Maxine and the tenets of sankofa, Black people can and do (re)claim time. These instances of temporal reclamation take on many forms. For the Black girls in this chapter, digital activism creates a pathway to temporal reclamation. Instead of waiting for a specific moment in the linear progression from childhood to adulthood, Black girl activists do not rely on age as the primary indicator of their readiness to fight for social justice. Instead, they "reposition themselves on the temporal spectrum" through community-based organizing efforts.[13] The Black girls discussed in this chapter place their own experiences of temporal disempowerment within a broader collective fight to make and reclaim time. Ultimately, Black girls' activist organizing, particularly in digital spaces, reflects BGA through creation of new temporal structures and realities for themselves.

#FreeGrace: Moving Black Girls from Afterthought to Forethought

Educational disparities and discrimination against Black girls in the United States have a well-documented history.[14] Black girls are more likely to be suspended from school than other races of girls and less likely to garner compassion from school personnel. The ethnographic and anecdotal experiences I share throughout this book speak to how even the most well-resourced schools are oftentimes hostile to Black girls.[15] These realities alone make primary and secondary schooling difficult for Black students, but the onset of the COVID-19 global pandemic compounded the level of disservice education systems do to Black girls. The case of fifteen-year-old Grace of Michigan shows how the pandemic, like most large-scale catastrophic events, further marginalized the most vulnerable.[16]

Throughout the spring of 2020, the rise in COVID-19 cases led to widespread school closings and transitioning to virtual school, including Grace's school district in Beverly Hills, Michigan. Many students across the country struggled with the switch to online learning, but virtual learning presented a distinct set of challenges for students with learning disabilities like Grace, who has ADHD. By law, public K–12 school systems must provide reasonable accommodations for students with disabilities as outlined in students' Individualized Education Plans (IEPs). As teachers struggled to adjust to teaching online, one could understand how the specificities of students' IEPs might have dropped from their radar, but such a shift in priorities would have had a significant impact on the students whose accommodations could not be facilitated properly in virtual learning environments. This is what happened to Grace; she did not receive the appropriate learning accommodations and therefore failed to complete her homework assignments. On May 15, 2020, a white judge, Mary Ellen Brennan, determined that Grace's failure to complete her homework provided reason enough to hold her in a juvenile detention center. At the time of Brennan's judgment, Grace had already been on probation for stealing and getting into a physical altercation with her mother. Though it seems preposterous that failure to submit homework could be considered a crime in any context, initially, Brennan said that Grace's failure to submit her work constituted a violation of her probation. However, when pressed, Brennan claimed that Grace's detention was not based solely on incomplete homework but instead implemented because she felt Grace posed a threat to her mother under the stay-at-home orders most states had adopted at that time. Grace's story galvanized communities to seek justice on her behalf.

Among those fighting for Grace were seventeen-year-olds Eva Oleita and Ama Russell, cofounders of the organization Black Lives Matter in All Capacities (BLMIAC). Russell and Oleita started BLMIAC in June 2020 as a way to draw attention to the plight of Black girls and women suffering (and dying) at the hands of racist policing systems, medical institutions, and education systems. When Oleita and Russell started BLMIAC, they did so in the wake of sociopolitical turmoil. At the time, people throughout the United States were organizing large rallies protesting police violence, including ones which called for the state of Kentucky to arrest the Louisville officers who killed Breonna Taylor while she slept in her home in a case of a no-knock warrant gone horribly wrong. In addition to the ongoing outcries against murderous police, COVID-19 cases continued to increase around the world, and the pandemic brought about its own set of racial injustices. BLMIAC came on the national news scene in response to these COVID-related injustices, specifically in defense of Grace.

At its core, Grace's story represents the temporal dispossession Black girls face as a result of disproportionate school suspensions and incarceration, early adultification, and higher exposure to interpersonal violence.[17] To bring attention to these aspects of Black girlhood along with Grace's specific plight, Oleita and Russell utilized digital resources coupled with the intensity of the moment. One of BLMIAC's primary avenues for organizing and generating awareness has been through Instagram. While the group's first official action was a #SayHerName march "dedicated to the Black women and girls victimized by police brutality," they built momentum around advocating for Grace's release in the weeks immediately following her detention.[18] Through their activist efforts, both online and in the streets, Oleita and Russell helped shed light on the full story of Grace's humanity. Using the hashtag #FreeGrace, they made a series of Instagram posts pointing out the cruelty of detaining a child with a documented disability (ADHD) in a criminal facility because of failure to complete homework in a virtual environment with no academic support during a global pandemic.[19] In this case, the school system committed the actual crime by failing to provide reasonable accommodations for Grace to complete her assignments. Yet the state portrayed Grace, a Black girl, as the criminal. This set of injustices pushed Oleita and Russell to advocacy, and the duo staged a sit-in at the Oakland County courthouse in Pontiac, Michigan, as their first action in support of Grace.[20] While convening with protesters in the physical space of the courthouse, Oleita and Russell also took to digital space to share their thoughts and motivations in an Instagram Live video. Even though the pair has several Instagram posts that speak to their mission, this thirteen-minute video offers an intersectional analysis of Black girlhood, naming the ways time works against Black girls. BLMIAC's strategy of naming reveals both the cyclical and agential natures of Black temporalities, serving as both a critique of and action against temporal dispossession.

Oleita and Russell identify erasure, criminalization, and misrepresentation as ongoing injustices against Black girls, and they use the word "afterthought" throughout the Live video to emphasize these injustices.[21] In the opening minutes of their dialogue, Russell explains, "As we fall victim to these systems who want us to become victims . . . Black girls, Black women—we become the afterthought . . . we the last people on everyone's mind."[22] They go on to say, "So, we wanna make sure that we're going hard for Grace" because "she is a person, and she's also a symbol for how Black girls are criminalized, Black girls are not treated with care, and Black girls are an afterthought." Not only do Oleita and Russell name the relegation of Black girls and women to a status of unimportance, but they also point out the effects of this subjugation. One effect is that Black girls "are always the bearer. [They] bear everything so that other people don't have to." Oleita and Russell's assessment of Black girls as the bearer speaks to how Black girls and women often form the frontlines in advocating for Black men and boys without reciprocation.[23] Even programs like Barack Obama's My Brother's Keeper initiative, which stem from the endangered Black male discourse that continues to have a stronghold on approaches to social policy, force Black girls to bear injustices in their assumptions that Black girls are (or will be) fine. The misguided notion that Black girls do not need the same attention and advocacy as Black boys in fights for social justice creates the conditions for Black girls to become "the most forgotten and neglected."[24] Being an afterthought constitutes a form of temporal dispossession that manifests as a lack of care and love for Black girls and women, which ultimately leads to their embodied and psychic deterioration.

Oleita and Russell also name early adultification as a threat to Black girls' well-being in their Instagram Live dialogue. As discussed throughout this book, people tend to see Black girls as more grown up than girls of other racial groups. This tendency results in biases that position Black girls as less innocent and therefore less likely to garner compassion. In Grace's case, Brennan's decision to prioritize the safety of Grace's *adult* mother over the needs of a fifteen-year-old *child* demonstrates the material impact of early adultification on Black girls.[25] Resisting adultification bias, Oleita and Russell emphasize that Grace "is a Black *child* who has been wronged by the system, who has fallen victim to the system." They add, "We are both two Black children as well; we are both Black girls, and we could as quickly be Grace."[26] These statements highlight the discrepancy between how children should be protected and how institutional racism and sexism routinely deny Black girls this level of security. Oleita and

Russell's acknowledgment that they could just as easily be in Grace's position speaks to lack of support as an everyday part of Black girlhood. Through sustained attention to Grace's childhood, Oleita and Russell further illustrate the inhumanity of her punishment. They also note how Grace's position as a child will have an impact on how she remembers her detention: "We want to give her the resources so that she can cope on the outside because this is a traumatic experience. She's probably gonna have PTSD. She's probably gonna have different disorders when she comes out."[27] Their emphasis on providing resources demonstrates both temporal awareness and an attempt to take charge of time: they want to mitigate the future mental health damage Grace will experience as a result of past and present trauma.

In addition to explaining how erasure and early adultification rob Black girls of time, BLMIAC identifies the role that criminalization plays in Black girls' temporal dispossession. In an attempt to paint herself as compassionate, Judge Brennan defended her decision to detain Grace out of concern for her well-being. However, Oleita and Russell expose the fallacy of this portrayal. For one, they note that detention centers do not operate as spaces of care, especially "when dealing with Black girls." They also point out how Brennan's use of Grace's prior convictions as evidence of criminality contradicts any claims of genuine consideration for her welfare. Russell explains, "If the judge was really trying to care for this Black girl, you would not—during that hearing—put all her business out in the public when the media is there." Oleita adds, "The only reason why the judge is bringing up all these prior convictions... is because she wants to turn the media and the public away from Grace.... She wants a fifteen-year-old girl to be slandered in the news media."[28] Brennan released information about Grace's record, knowing many people would not advocate for Grace if they felt like she had already solidified herself as a criminal. This strategy worked to an extent because some people walked back their initial support of Grace after finding out about her placement on probation for fighting with her mother and stealing. Oleita confirms, "I've seen it. I've seen people say, 'oh, well she must have done something bad, or she must have done this.'"[29] Along with the judge's hypocrisy, Russell and Oleita point out the racism undergirding Grace's circumstances: "If Grace was white, this would have never happened. She would have got the resources she needed back in November... back when she was [thirteen years old] using [stealing and fighting] as a cry for help."[30] Russell and Oleita's assessment of race-based outcomes extends beyond mere conjecture as Black girls do not have the same access to mental health resources and fall prey to the carceral system much more frequently than their white counterparts. Ultimately, by interpreting Grace's past actions as a cry for help instead of evidence of present criminality, Oleita and Russell demonstrate how white supremacist time works against Black girls.

Through BLMIAC, and specifically through their advocacy for Grace, Oleita and Russell utilized the connective and far-reaching qualities of the digital to deploy BGA toward shifting disempowering temporal landscapes in the following ways. First, they move Black girls from afterthought to forethought. After reminding their audience(s) how Black girls and women tend to fall by the wayside in dominant discourses and practices of activism, Oleita and Russell assert that they are "no longer standing for" this reality, explaining, "Black girls no longer need to be just put down to this supportive role. We deserve for people to fight for us, so that's exactly why we're out here fighting for Grace."[31] The girls actively take a stand to center Black girls in Black freedom organizing. Second, they take advantage of opportunities to help the living. Throughout the video the girls emphasize that they want to fight for Grace while she is still alive. They reflect upon how, far too often, people wait until it is too late to fight for Black girls; oftentimes when Black girls die as a result of social injustice(s), "it takes years for people to even start saying their name/protesting for them." As Oleita explains, "If we don't fight for her, Grace is like so many other Black kids who go through the system, but the only difference between Grace and all these other kids is that we're fighting for them right now." The emphasis on "right now" shows that they want to save Grace before she becomes a hashtag. To make her point, Oleita invokes the death of Breonna Taylor: "Grace is . . . a living person that we can fight for. Breonna Taylor: she got killed in her house back in March while she was sleeping, and . . . people are turning her name into some type of trend and into some type of meme." While BLMIAC acknowledges the importance of fighting for justice for Breonna Taylor's loved ones, they also realize that, ultimately, her life cannot be saved. In this realization, the girls allow for revering the dead while not losing sight of the urgency of helping those suffering in the present. Along these lines, BLMIAC claims childhood, and Black girlhood specifically, as a stage that should be marked by freedom. Oleita reminds people that "we can go home. . . . We can be on social media. We can be online. [Grace] doesn't have that freedom, and she's a child. These are prime years. These are fundamental years. And she needs this time right now." This sentiment reflects the everyday things that teenagers *should* be able to do and how Grace, along with other Black children who fall victim to social injustices, has been robbed of the opportunity to do those things. Fighting for the living means making sure Grace gets time to enjoy her childhood. Finally, Oleita and Russell work to change Black girls' relationship to the future. They use the history of Black girls as motivation to take control of the present so that more Black girls do not have to suffer or die from injustice in the future. Both girls' emphasis on fighting for Grace (and other Black girls) while she is still alive is a gesture of hope. Russell says: "After this, Grace will live a very successful life. Grace will prosper." This statement aims to speak a new future into existence, thus highlighting the key features of Black temporalities and exercising the inventive functions of BGA.

Being the Change: Marley Dias and #1000BlackGirlBooks

Using the past and the present to create different possibilities for the future not only defines Black temporalities but also marks a key component of Black girls' digital activism. Around the time I began researching Black girls' digital practices, I came across a trending hashtag on Twitter: #1000BlackGirlBooks. Often accompanying the hashtag were pictures of its then eleven-year-old founder, Marley Dias. Curious to learn more about Dias and her campaign, I clicked the hashtag, which led me to news stories, interviews, and other social media posts about the project. Dias founded #1000BlackGirlBooks out of her frustration with "never reading books about Black girls or any different type of character" besides white boys (and their dogs).[32] Channeling that frustration, Dias set out to collect one thousand books featuring Black girl protagonists with the goal of donating the books to schools. Dias's project appealed to me not only as a Black girlhood studies scholar but also as a former Black girl who had been reading for five whole years before I ever encountered a Black girl character in one of my books.[33]

Dias's conclusions about the books she read in school came from a place of personal experience, but her instincts about the lack of Black girls in her assigned reading represent a broader problem of racial and ethnic exclusion in K–12 education at the national level. Furthermore, even though Dias comes from a family who can afford to provide her with any types of books she wants, at eleven years old, she was already perceptive enough to realize that her frustration resulted from a larger systemic problem. Therefore, Dias chose to start #1000BlackGirlBooks with the goal of influencing curriculum on a national and global scale. In explaining her big-picture approach, Dias notes: "Teachers assign books that you must read. If those books are not diverse and do not show different people's experiences then kids are going to believe that there is only one type of experience that matters."[34] For Dias, "Black girl books are not just for black girls; they are for all children because not all black girl stories are the same."[35]

At first, #1000BlackGirlBooks might not seem to fit into the same discussion as Grace. After all, incarceration and its effects reflect much more drastic material conditions than being forced to read about white boys. However, Marley Dias's #1000BlackGirlBooks campaign connects to the work of organizations like BLMIAC in its resistance to white supremacist temporal dispossession. In fact, #1000BlackGirlBooks marks an even earlier intervention against devaluation and erasure that girls like Grace likely did not have. To be clear, I do not mean to suggest that reading books about Black girls would have prevented Grace (or another Black girl in her position) from falling victim to the criminal (in)justice system. However, given the connection between Black children's elementary school performance and future incarceration in a country that funnels Black children from schools to prisons, this kind of early intervention might have planted different kinds of seeds than the ones planted by the omission of Black girls' stories from school curricula.

Dias's #1000BlackGirlBooks campaign elucidates and operates according to the cyclical and agential natures of Black temporalities. At a fundamental level, #1000BlackGirlBooks ties together technologies of the past, present, and future. Dias's impetus to start the campaign came from one of the oldest media formats—the book—but she used (primarily) the power of new media technologies like Twitter to promote her campaign and collect well over ten thousand books for schools and libraries. Dias's vision for the campaign also reflects cyclical temporality. Her goals "to change the way we imagine black girls in books and in culture" and "create new spaces for black girls to be represented" hold the present and future together instead of presenting them as distinct points in a linear progression.[36] But beyond demonstrating the cyclical nature of Black time, Dias's campaign illustrates how Black girls develop a form of temporal agency through their digital activism. Part of the reason Dias developed the #1000BlackGirlBooks campaign is because she decided that she did not want to spend more time reading about white boy protagonists. For Dias, and other children who do not see themselves in their school reading assignments, the priority given to white boys' stories represents a temporal loss. Through starting #1000BlackGirlBooks, Dias reclaimed and refocused her time toward collecting books with Black girl main characters, a project that actively reshapes present and future learning possibilities for students in K–12 schools.

Since its launch in 2015, Marley Dias has catapulted #1000BlackGirlBooks to a multimedia, multiplatform campaign for Black girls' representation.[37] Within a year of starting #1000BlackGirlBooks, Dias landed a publishing opportunity with *Elle* magazine. During her guest editorship with *Elle*, which was the first of its kind, Dias put together an online zine for *Elle*'s website called *Marley Mag*. The zine features a range of content, including interviews with Misty Copeland, Hillary Clinton, Ava DuVernay, and Larry Wilmore. In the opening letter of the zine, Dias notes, "My passion for books has changed my life. Between school, homework, tests, and play time with my friends, I have worked my butt off to create this space where black girls' stories are read and celebrated in schools and libraries."[38] This accounting of Dias's activities reflects her temporal agency because she still found time to complete her schoolwork and play with her friends while trying to create a better educational experience for Black girls. After getting her feet wet with publishing *Marley Mag*, Dias went on to land a book deal with Scholastic. Her book *Marley Dias Gets It Done: And So Can You!* is part memoir, part how-to guide. In the book Dias tells the origin story of #1000BlackGirlBooks and the lessons she learned along the way. Dias concludes the text with the following message: "In many books when you get to the last chapter, it says 'the end.' But for me, my mission is an exciting new adventure that's at the very beginning—today, tomorrow, always. I'm just getting started! And so can you. Right now."[39] By concluding her book with a beginning, Dias further iterates Black time as cyclical. The end and beginning are not separate points on a line but rather simultaneous points in a continuous circle.

Marley Dias's journey from #1000BlackGirlBooks to becoming an author reflects BGA as a force of temporal restructuring in the following ways. First, Dias did not let age define when she would start her writing career. Though she went through traditional pathways to publishing, the digital helped facilitate her success in this arena. *Marley Mag* is a digital publication itself, but even *Marley Gets It Done* would not have come to fruition without the power of the #1000BlackGirlBooks hashtag. Another way that Dias's trajectory represents BGA lies in how Dias used #1000BlackGirlBooks to restructure her time. Dias had already reclaimed time she lost reading about white boys and their dogs by starting the hashtag. However, her use of this repossessed time holds just as much significance as its reclamation. Dias used her newly reclaimed time to become an author herself, thereby adding to the stories of Black girls. Dias has remained in public school even as she has risen to fame, which means she still has to meet certain curricular requirements. However, by working so hard to change curricula in her own school system and nationwide, Dias has reshaped what her time and other Black girls' time in school might look like. Furthermore, the work Dias has done and continues to do will undoubtedly shape her future in beneficial ways. Overall, Dias's #1000BlackGirlBooks campaign reflects temporal restructuring for the sake of a broader community rather than individual possession, and this restructuring exemplifies the creative force of BGA.

For those who might read Marley Dias's activism as an exception rather than an example that applies to quotidian Black girlhood, I turn to Savannah Shange's "Black girl ordinary." Shange, citing Lauren Berlant, defines Black girl ordinary as "a genre of crisis ordinary, which posits 'the ordinary as an impasse shaped by crisis in which people find themselves developing skills for adjusting to newly proliferating pressures to scramble for modes of living on.'"[40] In this framework, the ordinariness of crisis necessitates continuous creation of survival strategies. While Marley Dias's boredom with reading about white boys and their dogs may not constitute a crisis in itself, the lack of Black girl protagonists in schoolbooks does reflect the serious and persistent threat of Black girl erasure. Therefore, Dias's creation of #1000BlackGirlBooks functions as a survival tool—not necessarily Dias's individual survival but the collective survival of Black girls both within literature and in the broader cultural imaginary. Shange's elaboration on Black girl ordinary counters the temptation to write Dias's digital activism off as exceptional "Black girl magic":

> You might also know Black girl ordinary by her government name: #blackgirlmagic. A circulated, selfied, carefree mode of Black femininity, #blackgirlmagic has been both celebrated for its affirmation of Black women's thrival despite the adversities of racial capitalism and critiqued for its association with a light and curly stratum of bourgeois negroes. Black girl ordinary and #blackgirlmagic are coterminous; I use the former to center a materialist reading of gendered Black self-making and refuse the misogynoir that may seek to elide what is common to Black girls in order to elevate that which is seen as exceptional. We are conjurers, all—what's magical is that we are still here.[41]

In other words, the seemingly exceptional, magical tools Black girls create and deploy toward their survival become parts of ordinary, everyday Black girlhood. Therefore, Marley Dias's creation of the #1000BlackGirlBooks campaign is yet another example of Black girls doing what they always do (and have done): carving out spaces for themselves within and against the social structures that work so diligently toward their erasure. This creative, inventive impulse *is* BGA through and through.

Staking Claim: The Art Hoe Collective's Elevation of Marginalized Artists

Black girls use the digital to fight back against institutional racism and sexism in their everyday lives. While children in the United States spend much of their time in primary and secondary schools, other types of institutions can have just as much bearing on their subjective formation. Imagine a teenage Black girl who dreams of being a professional artist wandering through an exhibit at a local museum only to find no faces, bodies, or other subjective realities that look like hers. She could internalize this absence and begin to think that maybe art is not for her, that maybe her artwork will never make it to the walls of a gallery or famous museum. Instead, she takes out her cell phone, poses in front of one of the revered classical paintings, and snaps a selfie. She posts the selfie on Tumblr with #arthoe. But what is an "art hoe" anyway?

The Art Hoe Collective (AHC) was cofounded in 2015 by then fifteen-year-old genderqueer teen Mars and their partner Jam in an effort to showcase the art of queer people of color while simultaneously providing a space for creative and experiential expression of identity and self-acceptance. According to Mars, the art hoe movement is "an opportunity to shift paradigms and redefine blackness by challenging stereotypes about people of color."[42] While the collective, created by and for people of color (POC), aims to include a range of subjectivities, Mars has described the group as especially friendly to "non binary people of colour [sic] [who] don't really have a stable platform where they can prove and show what they're capable of without being questioned about their identity."[43] In addition to using visual imagery to challenge colonialist notions about what art is and who gets to be an artist, the name of the collective itself reclaims the word "hoe" as a subversive term. When asked about the choice to use the phrase "art hoe," Mars responded: "'Hoe' is AAVE (African American Vernacular English) and is normally a derogatory way to refer to women—especially Black women—as being promiscuous, within the male gaze," and "using the term in an arbitrary way diminishes its harmful origin in light of something better."[44] Another AHC member, Sage Adams, shared a similar philosophy of reclamation, arguing that "it's important that it's called art hoes because we wanted to define how we're being seen. So, we get to choose our narrative. We get to represent ourselves."[45]

The art hoe hashtag gained traction on Tumblr, a multimedia personal blogging site, but as the art hoe concept solidified from hashtag to movement to collective, its primary platform transitioned to Instagram. The reblogging feature of Tumblr played a role in the AHC choosing Instagram as its primary platform, with seven Black girls and enbies ranging in age from fifteen to twenty-four serving as curators.[46] In an interview with the now defunct blog *The Awl*, Adams explained how white girls appropriated the art hoe hashtag in ways that decentered and erased the queer, POC artists the collective aims to amplify.[47] While the AHC still uses Tumblr as a secondary platform, Instagram's inherently archival design makes it an apt site for the group to enact its curatorial mission. Instead of using a hashtag to compile the content from individual sites (as is the case with Tumblr), people interested in following the AHC as a group can simply visit their Instagram profile to find art associated with the collective displayed in one place. Additionally, the technical affordances of Instagram help to mitigate the hashtag appropriation that can occur on Tumblr, because only the AHC curators can post content on the group's Instagram account. The AHC has been intentional about seeking and sharing work of POC through its Instagram curation, which allows artists to submit their work for exhibition. In line with the mission of the collective, the Instagram gallery includes a range of media formats: photography, film, performance art, paintings, illustrations, and mixed-media pieces. By inviting work from queer artists of color, a group that inevitably includes Black girls, the AHC collects art as evidence of Black experiences.[48] Through an establishment of queer sensibilities and aesthetics as well as a commitment to counterhegemonic narratives about Black girlhood and Blackness in general, the Art Hoe Collective enacts a radical curatorial praxis that evinces both the nonlinear and agential qualities of Black temporalities.[49]

The AHC's gallery operates as a form of redress for the historical exclusion of Black and POC artists from hegemonic Western art. For one, the AHC confronts these institutional barriers by redefining what counts as art and who gets to make and exhibit art. When the art hoe movement first started, self-proclaimed art hoes would superimpose images of themselves (either through selfies or Photoshop) onto canonical art pieces. This self-insertion into classic paintings demonstrates a form of traveling to the past. Of course, the AHC cannot literally rewrite history, but this digital time travel allows for a correction of whitewashed historical art and art discourses. In this act, the AHC and its constituents both disrupt histories that have excluded them and create urgency around broader cultural conversations regarding artistic subjects, thereby reclaiming centuries of time stolen from Black artists and art subjects. In addition to claiming creative power to define art, the AHC circumvents institutional gatekeepers by creating a space for nonhierarchal community-building among queer artists of color. Through showcasing work by artists who range in experience from teens experimenting with smartphone cameras to professional filmmakers like Jenn Nkiru, the AHC not only breaks down barriers between amateur and professional but also utilizes the interactive functionality of Instagram in the interests of up-and-coming artists. This dissolution of generational barriers between veteran artists and newcomers reflects an interplay between the past, present, and future rather than a linear progression from young to old. Furthermore, by serving as a potential launching pad for new artists, the AHC can accelerate young Black artists' careers. The AHC's implementation of a microgrant initiative in 2020 has allowed the group to focus on this aspect of its mission even more. Each round of microgrant applications focuses on a specific demographic—Black trans women, queer nonwhite artists, and Asian Americans—and the recipients receive at least $500 (though the most recent rounds have offered $1,000 to each recipient). By giving direct aid to its constituents, the AHC provides a means for Black (and POC) artists to receive recognition in the present moment even, maybe especially, if they have not become famous in their fields yet. Through their acts of curation and community-building, the AHC disrupts exclusionary practices in institutional art, and this disruption embodies the creative, inventive forces of BGA.

Along with the agency embedded in the AHC's nonlinear temporality, the political commitments conveyed through the group's curatorial process reflect temporal reclamation. The AHC's work is partially about creating exposure for young artists of color, but the collective also promotes a message of self-love that is specifically about loving one's queerness. The AHC started with queer people of color in mind, which means they not only center traditionally marginalized artists but also create a space in which queer Black youth can be themselves in ways that might otherwise be discouraged. Through their curation, the AHC counters queer youth marginalization through discursive and material affirmation. These commitments make the AHC conducive to enactments of Black queer aesthetics. Black queer aesthetics encompass "practices of embodiment and rupture, where embodiment results from repeated gestures, acts, and interactions that reinscribe intangible beings into physical bodies and multiple layers of meaning into confined space, and rupture is the primary methodology of ontological reorientation in both time and space."[50] In other words, Black queer aesthetics are about creation and (re)configuration of time, space, and embodiment—a generative force for queer Black girls and all people of marginalized genders whose existence and cultural production(s) were "never meant to survive ... [and] perhaps also *never meant to appear*."[51] The AHC thwarts dominant society's attempts to repress and eradicate Black queer people by building and sustaining community through a publicly accessible curation of queer POC art. Instead of waiting for the world to catch up or offer validation, the AHC encourages queer self-love *now*. The way the AHC creates the conditions for queer self-love to thrive is an example of BGA.

Conclusion: Reinventing the Future

The very act of creation that BGA facilitates relies on alternative approaches to temporality beyond hegemonic, linear time. While Black girls' activism is clearly not a new phenomenon, understanding their organizing efforts as a product of BGA allows us to see how they are (re)inventing the future. For the girls I discuss in this chapter, and Black girl activists broadly speaking, the future is certainly not an abstract elsewhere but instead an integral component of their organizing efforts because they see the past, present, and future as inextricably linked.

Acts of reclamation—especially in the temporal sense—are critical to Black girls who have time taken away from them through early adultification, disproportionate school suspensions, high susceptibility to violence, and higher instances of incarceration. The way that Black girls stake claim to time through their activist organizing exemplifies what Tina Campt calls the "grammar of Black Feminist futurity," which describes "the power to imagine beyond current fact and to envision that which is not, but must be."[52] The activist work of Marley Dias, Eva Oleita, Ama Russell, and the Art Hoe Collective demonstrates how Black girls reclaim and repurpose temporality in ways that undermine temporal dispossession. In this way, these youths create a blueprint, or perhaps a Blackprint, for securing Black girl futures.

One of the main requirements for securing Black girl futures involves naming and dismantling the obstacles to Black girls' survival and well-being. A key first step in calling out the everyday challenges Black girls face to be acknowledged and protected involves being honest about Black girls' representation, which Marley Dias has done through her #1000BlackGirlBooks campaign and beyond. At an early age, Dias recognized the dearth of Black girl protagonists in her elementary school literature curriculum as an injustice. She knew that she deserved to see herself reflected in the literature but also that students of all backgrounds needed to be exposed to stories about Black girls. Dias's insistence on the value of Black girls' stories connects to the work of Eva Oleita and Ama Russell of BLMIAC because the same white supremacist forces that shape the institutional exclusion of Black girls from elementary curricula create the systemic conditions that emboldened a judge to incarcerate Grace instead of providing her with mental health resources. In their discussion of Grace, Oleita and Russell name Black girls' obstacles clearly: relegation to afterthought status, early adultification, and the school-to-prison pipeline. Their fight for Grace, and for the most marginalized groups within Black communities, is also a fight to dismantle the systems that uphold and perpetuate these obstacles. Likewise, both the artistic content and the political commitments of the AHC work to dismantle hegemonic gatekeeping standards within the world of art. In all three of these cases, Dias, Oleita, Russell, and the AHC speak truth to power and then act on those truths through their organizing efforts.

Along with naming and dismantling, processes of amplification and multiplication will be critical to creating and sustaining Black girl futures for the following reasons. First, in order to combat attempts at erasure, Black girls will need avenues through which their voices can be heard. Not only will Black girls need to vocalize (and otherwise document) their experiences, but their stories will need to be shared. For both BLMIAC and the AHC, the digital facilitates multiplicitous connection across space and time. When BLMIAC staged a sit-in to demand Grace's release, people gathered with them in the physical space of the courthouse grounds, but people also watched the video on Instagram Live, meaning that even people who were in different geographic locations or time zones could still participate in the action and, more importantly, spread the word about Grace. As a digital curation, the AHC has similar connective ability. The group has over 95,000 followers on Instagram and actively facilitates connections between AHC followers and professional artists in all stages of their careers. Additionally, as a publicly accessible account, the AHC's Instagram provides a way for a wide range of people to see the work of queer Black and POC artists. The work of BLMIAC and the AHC signals to the spatiotemporal power Black girls exhibit and claim through their digital content. Their methods of amplification and multiplication not only ensure that their voices are heard but also demonstrate how Black girls can use digital spaces to make their own demands on their own terms. While Oleita, Russell, and the AHC have been effective in using the digital to bolster their activism, if there were such a thing as an activist Cinderella story, Dias's #1000BlackGirlBooks campaign would be it. What started out as a hashtag morphed into book drives for schools throughout the United States and Jamaica (where Dias's parents were born), a guest editorship with *Elle* magazine in 2016, and a book contract with Scholastic in 2018. Most recently, Dias secured a deal with Netflix to host a read-along show called *Bookmarks*, which premiered in 2020. Dias still maintains her personal Instagram and Twitter accounts, but such an expansive digital platform not only allows her to inhabit spaces that have historically been denied to Black girls but also equips her with the tools to amplify and multiply Black girls' voices and stories in unprecedented ways.

Some might argue that Black girls having to fight for their survival robs them of their childhood. A version of this argument emerged when a fifteen-second video clip of seven-year-old Wynta-Amor Rogers shouting out "No justice, no peace" at a Black Lives Matter demonstration went viral. While some people hailed her as a hero, others lamented the fact that she could not have a carefree childhood and also cautioned against how such imagery perpetuates the strong Black girl/woman trope. While it is true that Black girls *should* be allowed to live carefree childhoods, it is also true that people who uphold white supremacist heteropatriarchy will rob Black girls of their childhood innocence whether they resist or not. Therefore, while Black girls' activism does not give them back their *innocence*, it does allow them at least some control of their *time*.

The project of creating and sustaining futures for Black girls will ultimately require ongoing imaginative and creative dexterity. Instead of renovating the "master's house," we have to tear it down altogether and build something anew, something that we have never seen before.[53] As Black feminist scholar Brittney Cooper explains, world-makers are those who "control the flow and thrust of history," in contrast to space-takers who "merely take up space to which they are not entitled."[54] Black girls' temporal agency, especially as exercised in digital spaces, positions them as world-makers by giving them the ability to manipulate time and space toward the goal of claiming and creating a sustainable future.

Conclusion
What Does Black Girl Autopoetics Make Possible?

In "Poetry Is Not a Luxury" Audre Lorde wrote, "But there are no new ideas still waiting in the wings to save us.... There are only old and forgotten ones, new combinations, extrapolations and recognitions from within ourselves—along with the renewed courage to try them out."[1] Black girl autopoetics offers us these new combinations, extrapolations, and recognitions of old ideas about Black life, especially in relation to geographies, archiving, self-expression, and time. To look at these features of Black life from the perspective of Black girls is an exercise imbued with possibility.

Black girl autopoetics gives us new ways to think about the relationship between Blackness and space. Certainly, cartographic processes are not exclusive to Black people, but for us, and especially for Black girls, the stakes of mapping are different. To understand Black life in the United States, one has to understand Black cartographies. From mapping escape routes in hairstyles and songs to learning which streets mark the boundaries of the Black section of town, for Black Americans, intricate knowledge of geographies and mapping have long been essential to survival. Looking at Black spatialities through the lens of BGA allows us to see how digital space can be used simultaneously to create personal autonomy and community. Throughout this text, we have seen how Black girls express themselves through their digital content and connect to like-minded people around the issues and identity categories that are important to them. To this end, Black girls' digital content shows how their subjectivities complicate spatial formations (or mapping of them). In other words, how Black girls conceptualize and move through space has direct connections to their lived experiences of categories like race, gender, age, class, and sexuality. In demonstrating how their processes of mapping involve layered interaction between the digital, physical, and conceptual, Black girls' digital practices make concrete the value and impact of digital space(s).

The way that Black Americans have had to approach space means that our maps have always included elements that are intangible or illegible to outsiders, yet the digital adds one more layer to Black cartographic practices. Not only does BGA allow us to see the physical, conceptual, and digital layers that constitute Black space, but it also offers potentially new ways of understanding the spatiality of the digital. Just like the *Green Book* created alternate maps for Black travelers, Black girls' digital mapping demonstrates how they navigate their worlds but in a way that is not accessible to everyone. In this way, BGA operates as a system of encoding; Black girls create encoded maps through their digital content, and breaking the code requires cultural or ethnographic knowledge. These cartographies, hidden in plain sight, allow Black girls to create alternative spaces for themselves.

This practice of creating alternative spaces stimulates new ways of thinking about how to claim, occupy, navigate, and make spaces, signaling toward a conceptualization of spatial empowerment that undermines displacement. To be clear, I am not saying that utilizing digital platforms will negate or compensate for forces like gentrification and other forms of spatial injustice in the physical. Instead, I am saying that paying attention to how Black girls deploy BGA to create spaces for themselves might be instructive in how we understand space (and its layers), which seems to be a key first step in spatial repossession and expansion.

Like space, memory comprises a central element of Black life. For Black Americans, the fight to preserve personal and collective memory is tied up with both recuperation and survival as historical practices of violent erasure present unique obstacles to knowing the histories of our ancestors. Black girl autopoetics, as manifested in Black girls' digital practices, reinvigorates urgencies around preserving Black memory. Black girls' use of social media platforms to narrativize and archive important milestones and experiences speaks to the role of these practices in preserving Black memory. In this way, their digital practices correspond to both a history of Black vernacular photography and an urgency around documenting the moment.

Even though Black girls' digital content reinforces long-established conclusions about the need to preserve Black memory, looking at processes of archiving and documenting through the lens of BGA also compels us to reevaluate archival processes. For instance, Black girls' digital archives shift our thinking around what archives are and who holds responsibility for building and maintaining them. Despite the ephemerality of social media archives like Instagram profiles or YouTube channels, Black girls' curation of their experiences on these platforms draws attention to stories that add to the chronicles of Black life. If anything, the potential ephemerality of these sites creates even greater urgency around preserving the stories contained within them. This newfound understanding of social media's archival potential then leads us to take children more seriously as stewards of Black memory. That does not mean that we do not need professional archivists and historians. However, we cannot categorically dismiss the content of Black girls (and Black children in general) from the social history of Black life and memory.

Taking on this more expansive understanding about the composition of archives and the people responsible for building them means that we can have more robust collections of stories and experiences that document Black life. Such an approach would offer even more fuel in the fight against erasure. Additionally, understanding Black girls' digital content as archival might inspire new solutions for long-term preservation. Once we recognize the value of Black girls' online archives, then we can begin figuring out how to preserve these stories outside of corporate entities whose capacity for preservation only stretches as far as their profit margins.

In addition to battling for spaces to exist and fighting to preserve Black memory, representation remains key to Black life. For one, representation lies at the heart of Black Americans' struggle for recognition as humans. In this struggle, gaze plays a crucial part in understanding how representation corresponds to Black people's perceived (in)humanity. At the same time, Black people have long realized there can be no true recognition of Black humanity under a white supremacist, capitalistic gaze. Therefore, Black people must rely on self-definition as a resistance to dehumanization. In defining ourselves, Black people experience our humanity from a place of internal assuredness as opposed to external validation. For Black girls, processes of self-definition are complicated by intragroup pressures to be respectable.

One way that Black girls engage in processes of self-definition is through their digital content. As a whole, Black girls sharing their lives online adds to the body of knowledge about infinitely diverse Black experiences. However, despite the documentary potential of Black girls' digital content, Black girls run the risk of becoming hyper(in)visible as a result of their online activity, especially in sociocultural contexts that already position Black girls as unworthy of empathy and compassion. For Black girls who transgress the boundaries of respectable presentation, the intensity of hyper(in)visibility increases. Black girls who embody ratchet performativity, who post sexualized images of themselves, and who show off on social media are even more susceptible to hyper(in)visibility and its consequences. So, when Black girls make *themselves* hypervisible by engaging in these behaviors, they are not doing so out of naive misunderstanding of how their images travel or how people read them. Instead, their deliberate hypervisibility operates as blatant opposition to the people who would justify their denigration and dehumanization based on their digital content. In this way, BGA empowers Black girls to both define themselves and take up space in subversive ways.

Black girls who make themselves hypervisible through ratchet, sexual, and immodest behavior refract the gaze of misogynoir. Understanding Black girls' deliberate hypervisibility as a tool of self-definition bound up in refusal allows us to interrogate the function(s) of the gaze more deeply. In other words, Black girls' refusal to accommodate white supremacist, sexist expectations of how they should look and behave pushes us to reevaluate which gaze matters, to whom, and why. These questions also force us to grapple with how we assign value to Black girls based on their identity categories, especially at the intersection of race, gender, class, and sexuality. Provided we can work through the discomfort of this confrontation, then Black girls' self-definition in hypervisibility opens up possibilities for releasing ourselves from the notion that supposedly appropriate or correct representation will evince Black humanity. Instead, we can relinquish the burdens of propriety and commit to protecting all Black life, not just respectable Black life.

Like space, memory, and representation, temporality plays an integral role in Black American life. Whether through past centuries of enslavement or contemporary instances of state-sanctioned violence, Black Americans have had to race against time. While it is clear to see how white supremacy robs Black Americans of time, that does not mean time cannot be repossessed. Black people already have ways of undermining Western temporal structures, such as operating on CP time.[2] At the heart of CP time lies a prioritizing of community and sociality rather than capitalistic productivity and profit. Alongside this tried-and-true method of temporal subversion, BGA provides even more ideas and configurations for reclaiming and restructuring time.

For Black girls, digital activism functions as a tool for both responding to social injustices and using BGA to (re)structure and (re)create time. The Black girl activists whose stories appear in this book have used online platforms to raise awareness and make material changes within institutions that have historically robbed Black girls of time. In doing so, these girls have taken control over time, both personally and for their communities. In this way, they take back time that has been stolen from Black girls through forces like early adultification and the school-to-prison pipeline. Once they reclaim this stolen time, they restructure it in service of organizing and affecting change. Ultimately, Black girls' digital activism, as an instrument of BGA, demonstrates their efforts to (re)shape the future.

Further Explorations of Black Girl Autopoetics

Even though this text has used Black girls' digital content to highlight the salient features of Black girl autopoetics, its value and functions extend beyond the digital realm. Future research incorporating BGA might examine how it manifests in a range of sociocultural contexts. For instance, what kinds of artistic techniques might Black girls be innovating or transforming through BGA? Since art already serves as a creative product, avenues for Black girls' artistic expression—such as dance, theater, visual art, music, and creative writing—offer fruitful sites to explore what (else) BGA shows us about Black girlhood and Black life. Another place to consider the workings of BGA is school. Through the girls in this text, especially with the girls at Liberty Prep, we see how BGA allows Black girls to create alternate spaces in response to the restrictions of their physical school environments. One suggestion for future research would be to see how Black girls deploy BGA *within* schools. How do Black girls engage BGA to shape curriculum, create enrichment activities, and build relationships with their peers and teachers? Along these lines, Black girls might also use BGA to develop their own, likely informal, school or educational spaces.

Given the detrimental impact of misogynoir on Black girls' well-being, examining BGA at the intersection of Black girls' health and wellness also presents an opportunity for future research. Uneven access to health-care resources and unequal treatment within health-care systems remains a persistent problem for Black girls (and women). Looking at BGA in conjunction with health and wellness will offer insight into the creative strategies Black girls (could) enlist to support their own well-being along with the health and well-being of their peers and elders.

Finally, we return to Black girls' play as a site of BGA. The moment that inspired the research presented throughout this text came from reflecting on how Black girls spent their leisure time. In the scene that appears in the book's introduction, my cousins used digital technologies as part of their playtime, but they also regularly played with dolls and constructed imaginary worlds. Watching what and how Black girls play is like peering through a window to their imaginations. Therefore, further research on BGA might consider how the imaginative capacity reflected in Black girls' play corresponds to the creation and sustainability of Black life.

Agency and Possibility

This text has been in the making, even before I knew it, over the course of a decade. In that span of time, I have watched many of the Black girls whose stories appear in these pages grow up. Some have gone to and finished college, some have started or completed advanced degrees, some have their own businesses, and some are parents to little Black girls now. Some keep in contact through texts, phone calls, and lunch meetups. Others show love on Instagram or Facebook (which I realize means they look at me as one of the "old" folks in their lives). Watching these girls grow up has been an absolute joy, not only because of the sentimentality of the experience but also because their transition into adulthood means they have survived.

Collective Black survival lies at the heart of Black girl autopoetics as an instrument of agency and possibility. Black girl autopoetics offers us new ways of feeling old ideas about Black space, memory, representation, and time.[3] Reevaluating how we understand these key features of Black life through Black girls' agential production might make it possible for us to repurpose space and time toward our own survival. Here, I do not conflate survival with barely hanging on but instead invoke Alexis Pauline Gumbs's description of survival (via Audre Lorde) as "living in the context of what we have overcome... life after disaster, life in honor of our ancestors, despite the genocidal forces worked against them specifically so we would not exist."[4] Ultimately, Black girl autopoetics is a praxis of creation, and if Black girls can create the conditions for their survival while facing anti-Black heterosexist patriarchy, then what else is possible? Transformation? Fulfilled hopes and dreams? Black futures? Let's truly know, hear, support, and love Black girls, and we will see.

Notes

INTRODUCTION

1. Triller is a social media platform that allows users to make their own music videos using popular songs.
2. Collins, *Black Feminist Thought*.
3. Even though both Darnella Frazier and Judeah Reynolds witnessed George Floyd's murder, I focus on Frazier throughout the rest of the introduction. In doing this, I do not mean to imply that Reynolds's role was any less significant, but the backlash that Frazier received after posting the video of Floyd's murder online exemplifies the conditions under which Black girls participate in digital discourses.
4. Police violence against civilians also disproportionately affects Indigenous people and non-Black people of color, but I focus on Black people in my explanation here because the people I am talking about (Darnella Frazier and George Floyd) are Black and because the information cycle that informs Frazier's and Floyd's stories focuses most of its attention on Black victims of police violence.
5. Epko, "17-Year-Old Who Recorded George Floyd's Murder."
6. While news sources have not reported the identities of the people who bullied Frazier, it would not be unreasonable to assume that the trolls came from a wide range of racial and ethnic backgrounds. From an anecdotal perspective, Black people make up the majority of people I am connected to on social media, and I saw several people who shared a post that read: "If I ever get attacked by the police, don't record me, help me!" While this was not directly attacking Frazier, sharing it in the wake of Floyd's murder was an indirect way of judging Frazier. Days later, I saw more people

posting about Frazier's trauma and defending her, but the damage had already been done.

7   Quoted in Epko, "17-Year-Old Who Recorded George Floyd's Murder."
8   There are ways to get around this, but people have reported Facebook reprimanding them for using a name that does not match their "official" name.
9   Noble, *Algorithms of Oppression*.
10 *Misogynoir* is a term coined by Moya Bailey that refers to the distinct hatred of Black women and girls. See Bailey, *Misogynoir Transformed*.
11 Black women did come to Frazier's defense, touting her as a hero, but Frazier received the backlash before being hailed a hero. Frazier's heroic act was eventually recognized in a more mainstream way when she received a special Pulitzer award on June 11, 2021. See "Darnella Frazier," The Pulitzer Prizes, accessed March 8, 2023, https://www.pulitzer.org/winners/darnella-frazier.
12 Benjamin, *Race after Technology*, 69.
13 Noble, *Algorithms of Oppression*.
14 Gaunt, "The Disclosure, Disconnect, and Digital Sexploitation of Tween Girls' Aspirational YouTube Videos."
15 Weisbard, "Kyra Gaunt, on Played."
16 Gaunt, "The Disclosure, Disconnect, and Digital Sexploitation of Tween Girls' Aspirational YouTube Videos."
17 See Driscoll, *Feminine Adolescence in Popular Culture and Cultural Theory*; and Simmons, *Crescent City Girls*.
18 Berger, *Ways of Seeing*; Williams, "Structures of Feeling."
19 Bailey, "#transform(ing)DH Writing and Research"; Dill, "Poetic Justice."
20 I prefer the term *discussion groups* to *focus groups* because it feels more age-appropriate for the girls I engaged using this method.
21 I used the 2010 US Census data along with the yearly estimates provided by the US Census Bureau.
22 At the time I began this study, 2010 was the most recent census collection year. The 2020 census was still in progress at the time I began writing this book. While the data from that census will be available by the time this book is published, it was not available to me during my analysis.
23 Detroit, Michigan, appears on both lists, so that is why there are not twenty total cities.
24 Wynter, "Ethno or Socio Poetics," 87.
25 Wynter, "Ethno or Socio Poetics," 87.
26 Thomas, "PROUD FLESH Inter/Views."
27 McKittrick, *Sylvia Wynter*, 32.
28 McKittrick, *Dear Science*, 2.
29 Fanon, *Black Skin, White Masks*.
30 McKittrick, *Dear Science*, 136, 138.
31 Lorde, "A Litany for Survival."
32 Durham, *Home with Hip Hop Feminism*, 2.
33 Cox, *Shapeshifters*; Brown et al., "Doing Digital Wrongly."

34 Boylorn, "On Being at Home with Myself," 49.
35 For more on the development of Black girlhood studies as a field, see C. Owens et al., "Towards an Interdisciplinary Field of Black Girlhood Studies"; and Halliday, *The Black Girlhood Studies Collection*.
36 Jordan-Zachery and Harris, *Black Girl Magic beyond the Hashtag*, 6.
37 Jordan-Zachery and Harris, *Black Girl Magic beyond the Hashtag*, 15.
38 Jordan-Zachery and Harris, *Black Girl Magic beyond the Hashtag*, 15.
39 Of course, this does not mean there are no Black girls who identify with #BlackGirlMagic; I'm just pointing out how the girls in this specific study responded to it.
40 Brown, "Questions Regulate/Knowledge Radiates."
41 Smith, "Theorizing Black Girlhood."
42 The distinction between the experiences of girls and women played a critical role in the establishment of girls' studies and girlhood studies. Girls' agency in theorizing their own lives and bringing attention to their stories along with increased attention to girls as a consumer market contributed to the development and expansion of girls' studies. For more about the development of girls' and girlhood studies, see Kearney, "Coalescing."
43 O'Grady, "Olympia's Maid."
44 boyd, *It's Complicated*; Thiel-Stern, *From the Dance Hall to Facebook*; Banet-Weiser, "Am I Pretty or Ugly?"
45 Kearney, *Girls Make Media*, 3.
46 Mazzarella, *Girl Wide Web 2.0* and *The Mediated Youth Reader*.
47 LaBennett, *She's Mad Real*; Love, *Hip Hop's Lil' Sistas Speak*.
48 Baker, Staiano, and Calvert, "Digital Expression among Urban, Low-Income African American Adolescents"; Stokes, "Representin' in Cyberspace."
49 Lindsey, "'One Time for My Girls'"; Projansky, *Spectacular Girls*; Everett, "Have We Become Post-racial Yet?"
50 Brown, *Hear Our Truths*; Cox, *Shapeshifters*; Chatelain, *South Side Girls*; Simmons, *Crescent City Girls*.
51 Wade, "Not New to This."
52 I use the African American Vernacular English (AAVE) spelling of this word to emphasize its specific connections to hip-hop culture.

INTERLUDE

1 "Shook" is an AAVE colloquialism used to indicate fear.
2 The establishment of institutional review boards was part of the National Research Act of 1974, which Congress passed after the atrocities of the Tuskegee Syphilis Study went public.
3 Luke, "Digital Ethics Now," 87.
4 Floridi, "Digital Ethics Online and Off."
5 I use this phrasing because throughout my childhood my immediate family transitioned in and out of poverty (as defined by federal income standards). We lived in Section 8 housing at times, and my mom received SNAP benefits (aka food stamps) at

times. Even once she no longer qualified to receive those forms of assistance, which would suggest a change in socioeconomic status, she still supplemented her income with high-interest personal loans and credit cards. So that debt made it more difficult to escape poverty altogether.

6   The explanation about participating in the research or not and the ability for girls to decide which questions to answer are part of the IRB's requirements for conducting research with human participants.
7   Liberty Prep was an all-Black school at the time I began my research. I worked with the school's scheduler to ensure that only girls would be enrolled in the course since the research focuses on Black girls. I offer extensive details about this experience in chapter 1, but for this interlude, I focus only on the ethical concerns related to my positionality as a volunteer teacher.
8   Jackson, "We Need to Talk about Digital Blackface in Reaction GIFs"; Noble, *Algorithms of Oppression*; Browne, *Dark Matters*; Benjamin, *Race after Technology*.
9   Johnson and Nuñez, "Alter Egos and Infinite Literacies, Part III."
10 The privacy settings for YouTube differ from other major social media networks. In order to make a video "private" on YouTube, you must choose to make it unsearchable. However, this does not ensure total privacy because people with the link can still access the video even if the user did not give them the link.
11 Noble, *Algorithms of Oppression*; Gaunt, "The Disclosure, Disconnect, and Digital Sexploitation of Tween Girls' Aspirational YouTube Videos."

1. PLACES TO BE

1   I use quotation marks here because even my backup plan was ambitious and unrealistic.
2   This is what one of the students called me. Her actual mother referred to two of the girl's other Black teachers and me as her "comothers."
3   I use the word *diverse* loosely because the school's population was overwhelmingly white, and I had white students who stopped by my room periodically. But many of the Black, Latina, and Asian students visited with me during the school day.
4   They even taught me how to do "the Wobble" in preparation for my wedding reception.
5   People posed this question (or variations of it) to my students and me on more than one occasion. One particularly memorable time, I was outside with two of my Black girl students talking and laughing while standing under my umbrella. I cannot recall the topic of our conversation, but I do recall one of my white colleagues walking by and joking, saying: "You three look like you're up to something."
6   McKittrick, *Demonic Grounds*; Eaves, "Black Geographic Possibilities."
7   Butler, "Black Girl Cartography"; Cahill, "BlackGirl Geography," 59.
8   Eaves, "Black Geographic Possibilities," 81. For examples of these analyses, see Brown, *Hear Our Truths*; Cox, *Shapeshifters*; Butler, "Black Girl Cartography"; Cahill, "BlackGirl Geography."
9   Crowe and Bradford, "'Hanging Out in Runescape"; Ruckenstein, "Spatial Extensions of Childhood"; boyd, *It's Complicated*; Crenshaw, Ocean, and Nanda, "Black

Girls Matter." Research done by the African American Policy Forum and the Georgetown Center on Poverty and Inequality demonstrates how Black girls' suspension and expulsion rates not only criminalize them disproportionately but also make them more susceptible to interpersonal violence. Also see Morris, "'Ladies' or 'Loudies'"; Morris, *Pushout*.

10 Examples of these supposed transgressions that appeared in high-profile news stories include the Black girl from Spring Valley High School in South Carolina who was slammed to the ground by a white police officer (who faced no charges for his actions) and the Black girl from McKinney, Texas, Dejerria Becton, who was slammed to the ground by a white male police officer after someone called the police about Black children having a pool party. Also see Saar et al., *The Sexual Abuse to Prison Pipeline*; Epstein, Blake, and Gonzalez, *Girlhood Interrupted*.

11 Simmons, *Crescent City Girls*, 28.

12 Simmons, *Crescent City Girls*, 28.

13 Here, I use *re-present* to emphasize how people use digital technologies to reflect their own experiences (as opposed to seeing [or not seeing] themselves) represented in mainstream popular media. I discuss the differences between representation and re-presentation more in chapter 2.

14 Elwood, "Digital Geographies," 3.

15 I used ethnographic notetaking and digital audio recording to capture these conversations. In all conversations, the girls understood my research, and in the audio recorded conversations, I made them aware of and obtained their consent to use a digital recorder.

16 Richmond has five main neighborhoods: the East End, West End, Northside, Southside, and the Fan/Museum district. Of these neighborhoods, the East End and the Southside are seen as the least desirable neighborhoods, though both are being gentrified.

17 This was true at the time of writing this text, but one of these projects has been demolished, and the others will likely meet the same fate by the time this book is published.

18 In April 2019, community members opened a grocery store called 25th and Market as a way of addressing the lack of grocery options in the East End, particularly in Church Hill. Based on customer feedback about prices in the store being too high, it is unclear what the lasting impact of this store will be on the neighborhood(s) it serves.

19 Rockett and Williams, "Wave of Violence Continues in Richmond with 22 People Slain in the Past Two Months."

20 This is not necessarily standard practice for K–12 schools as a whole, and there was an official vetting process for volunteers who came to campus.

21 Since I was a volunteer, I did not spend extra time at the school attending faculty meetings or other professional development activities. Therefore, I do not have extensive knowledge of which elective teachers were volunteers and which ones were on payroll.

22 It took everything in me to control my facial expressions when she made this statement.

23 For ethical reasons, I could not compel the girls to participate in the research even if they were members of the class. I made this very clear in the consent forms that their parents signed. All of them elected to participate in the research.

24 I did include some tutorials but did not focus on this a great deal because it wasn't really the overall objective of the research.

25 Morris, *Pushout*; Crenshaw, Ocean, and Nanda, "Black Girls Matter"; Epstein, Blake, and Gonzalez, *Girlhood Interrupted*.

26 New You Brands, "Girls from around the World Participated in Live Conversation Featuring First Lady Michelle Obama."

27 For more about Black girls' susceptibility to sexual violence, see Saar et al., *The Sexual Abuse to Prison Pipeline*.

28 My use of *boy* here does not reflect a heteronormative assumption that girls only go to school dances with male dates. Instead, the girls only talked to me about heterosexual dating, so I do not have a sense of how or if their understandings of dating and consent might apply beyond heterosexual contexts.

29 She actually used the term *feminism*; that is not my projection.

30 For example, Black women who have blue (or other "unnatural") colored hair are oftentimes called "ghetto" or "unprofessional," while white women who wear similar hair colors are seen as "edgy" or "free spirits."

31 Miley Cyrus, Kim Kardashian, and Jennifer Lopez are a few famous examples.

32 While I was not familiar with Charlotte E. Jacobs's "critical feminist media pedagogy for Black girls" at the time I taught the Digital Expressions course, the girls' assessment of cultural appropriation reflects their development of an oppositional gaze. See Jacobs, "Developing the 'Oppositional Gaze.'"

33 West Academy includes prekindergarten through twelfth grade.

34 This is also a pseudonym.

35 Starting in seventh grade, each West Academy student receives a school-issued MacBook, which is covered in the cost of tuition.

36 Even though the girls I conversed with online (who represent cities throughout the United States) are not the subject of this chapter, Trump's election came up in the majority of those conversations too. Black girls across the country were worried about what his administration meant for their futures and the futures of people they care about.

37 I also discuss McKittrick's theory of garreting in "Indigo Child Runnin' Wild." Thanks to Nikol Alexander-Floyd for giving me this language.

38 McKittrick, *Demonic Grounds*, 29.

39 McKittrick, *Demonic Grounds*, 29.

40 boyd, *It's Complicated*, 61.

41 Hine, "Rape and the Inner Lives of Black Women," 912.

42 boyd, *It's Complicated*, 203.

43 I use quotation marks here because nothing truly disappears from the internet, but the Snapchat interface allows users to see stories and updates for only twenty-four hours.

44 Instagram has added a "Stories" feature since I originally conducted this research. Stories function similarly to snaps in the sense that they are available for twenty-

four hours. In more recent exchanges with Black girls (in 2020), several of them mentioned that they like making stories on Instagram more than posting pictures or videos to their profile. For them, the stories seem more immediate and timely.
45 Hine, "Rape and the Inner Lives of Black Women."
46 Squires, "Rethinking the Black Public Sphere."
47 Steele, "The Digital Barbershop"; Steele, "Black Bloggers and Their Varied Publics."
48 In independent schools, "upper school" is high school. So there were three Black girls in Jasmine's entire high school, which totals approximately two hundred students.
49 Jarmon, *Black Girls Are from the Future*.
50 One anecdotal example of this type of exchange comes from an instance when I workshopped a version of this chapter with a group of Black studies scholars. One of the main points of feedback that I received is that by focusing on the intersection of Black life and digitality, my work relies too heavily on the abstract. When I argued that the digital is geographical, I was told that was a nice slogan for a T-shirt or bumper sticker but that my work had not adequately proven that the digital is in fact geographical. The fact that many of my colleagues in this context took my assertion as an opinion, which I then had to prove, rather than a legitimate epistemological approach is illustrative of the persistent dichotomy of "online" versus "in *real* life."

2. "YOU GOTTA SHOW YOUR LIFE"

I use pseudonyms for the girls with whom I did participant observation and focus groups. I also use pseudonyms for the schools and organizations where I met with them. For the virtual ethnography, even though I only used public accounts, I still use pseudonyms out of respect for girls' future desire to change the public nature of their accounts.

1 I use this term in quotation marks because it is a problematic way that people describe (especially Black) girls who go through puberty early.
2 O'Grady, "Olympia's Maid."
3 Liberty Prep is a pseudonym. This is the same school that I discuss at length in chapter 1 of this book.
4 I make this distinction following Kara Keeling (citing Gayatri Spivak and Karl Marx). Representation refers to a proxy, or stand-in, while re-presentation is a portrait or replica. For instance, a character on a television show might represent Black girls with kinky hair. She stands in for other girls who look like her or whose experiences resemble her own. Re-presentation, however, would be a Black girl posting a selfie on social media because she is showing us a portrait of *her own* life. See Keeling, *The Witch's Flight*.
5 Trauma porn refers to content that bases its entertainment value almost exclusively on (oftentimes gratuitous) displays of trauma.
6 Morris, *Pushout*; Shange, *Progressive Dystopia*.
7 Hill, "Disturbing Disparities," 59.
8 Shange, *Progressive Dystopia*; Morris, *Pushout*; Crenshaw, Ocean, and Nanda, "Black Girls Matter."

9 Crenshaw, Ocean, and Nanda, "Black Girls Matter"; see also Hill, "Disturbing Disparities."
10 Campt, *Image Matters*, 7.
11 Wade, "Indigo Child Runnin' Wild."
12 Ruffin, "Digital Archives."
13 Trouillot, *Silencing the Past*.
14 My great-great-grandmother (born in the 1860s) only acknowledged and celebrated the birthday that was recorded for her in our family Bible because she did not have a birth certificate.
15 Campt, *Image Matters*; Thompson, *Shine*.
16 Wallis and Willis, *African American Vernacular Photography*, 9.
17 Cobb, *Picture Freedom*.
18 Wallis and Willis, *African American Vernacular Photography*, 9.
19 Certainly, there are popular brands of cell phones that cost more than computers, but excluding those brands, one could get a high-functioning smartphone for under fifty dollars.
20 Campt, *Image Matters*, 14.
21 Brown, *Hear Our Truths*.
22 Senft and Baym, "What Does the Selfie Say?," 1589.
23 Izadi, "Why #BlackOutDay Took Over Social Media."
24 "#TheBlackout—Home of Blackout Day."
25 Curly hair would be considered 3A–3C on the hair texture chart. Kinky hair, also derogatorily referred to as *nappy hair*, is 4A–4C. Many women with group 4 hair have reclaimed the term *nappy* as a source of pride, but it is still considered a derogatory term when used to describe someone else's hair.
26 This quote comes from an Instagram post within the Art Hoe Collective's curated collection. The Art Hoe Collective has since deleted its Instagram account.
27 Instagram Post, Art Hoe Collective (deleted).
28 Unless otherwise indicated, quotes from social media posts are anonymous, including when I have used pseudonyms to simulate anonymity.
29 These classifications are based on the Andre Walker Hair Typing System. While Walker has come under fire for making controversial comments about "kinky" hair texture, his hair typing system is still the go-to reference for describing hair texture groups.
30 Senft and Baym, "What Does the Selfie Say?"
31 Ladner, *Tomorrow's Tomorrow*.
32 Morris, *Pushout*.
33 Epstein, Blake, and Gonzalez, *Girlhood Interrupted*.
34 "Baby hairs" refers to edges that are styled in a way that look like a Black baby's hair.
35 While a discussion of masculine Black girls might seem to conflict with my previous arguments about denial of femininity to Black girls and women, there is a difference between choosing masculine gender expression for oneself and being relegated to masculinity (or the unfeminine) by external, societal forces and norms.
36 Brock, *Distributed Blackness*.
37 Williams, *Self-Taught*.

38   This connotation of white clothing is why many Black Americans wear white at funeral services and refer to them as "homegoing" services, a cause to celebrate rather than mourn.
39   The motivation behind Michelle Obama's national signing day comes from wanting to highlight all students who are attending college. Before her campaign, "signing day" was a specific celebration for student athletes signing to Division 1 universities.
40   The challenge is named after the song in the background, which is "Don't Rush" by Young T and Bugsey.
41   See the ongoing critiques of Black excellence in popular media: Ford, "Bel-Air and the Flawed Logic of 'Black Excellence'"; Underwood, "Is Black Excellence Killing Us?"; Asare, "Our Obsession with Black Excellence Is Harming Black People."
42   Bradley, *Chronicling Stankonia*.
43   Wallis and Willis, *African American Vernacular Photography*, 10.
44   Wallis and Willis, *African American Vernacular Photography*, 10.
45   Cruz, "LGBTQ Youth of Color Video Making as Radical Curriculum," 453, 456.
46   Lewis, "Pushing the Limits in Black Girl–Centred Research."
47   Campt, *Image Matters*, 5.
48   Pritchard, *Fashioning Lives*, 34.
49   Hernandez, *The Aesthetic of Excess*.
50   Campt, *Image Matters*, 6.
51   Wade, "Not New to This."
52   Morgan, "Archives and Histories of Racial Capitalism," 154.

3. "I LOVE POSTING PICTURES OF MYSELF!"

1   This is Bella's description. Bella, Instagram direct message to author, April 28, 2018.
2   Jessica, personal communication, August 1, 2017.
3   Instagram does have a "stories" feature that allows users to post supplemental content that disappears after twenty-four hours. Even though this feature was available when I started my research, it did not become popular among my research participants until years after it was introduced.
4   In AAVE, "extra" denotes excess in a way that often implies a state of being, as in when someone says, "She is so extra." The term is usually not meant as a compliment. A person who is extra is seen as demanding, transgressive, and a nuisance.
5   Love, "A Ratchet Lens."
6   Stallings, "Hip Hop and the Black Ratchet Imagination"; Cooper, "(Un)Clutching My Mother's Pearls."
7   Fleetwood, *Troubling Vision*; Hernandez, *The Aesthetics of Excess*.
8   Brock, *Distributed Blackness*, 129.
9   Cooper, "(Un)Clutching My Mother's Pearls," 218.
10 Stallings, "Hip Hop and the Black Ratchet Imagination"; Love, "A Ratchet Lens"; Tolliver, "Breaking Binaries"; Brock, *Distributed Blackness*.
11 Cooper, Morris, and Boylorn, *The Crunk Feminist Collection*; Meggs, "Is There Room for the Ratchet in the Beloved Community?"

12 Bradley, "To Sir, with Ratchety Love."
13 Mercer, "Black Hair/Style Politics"; Rooks, *Hair Raising*; Banks, *Hair Matters*; Craig, *Ain't I a Beauty Queen*.
14 Walker's pomades tend to be misrepresented as hair straightening formulas in Black popular culture even though Walker emphasized their therapeutic functions and tried to distinguish her product from hair straighteners. See Wilson, "Beauty Rites." For the CROWN Act, see Crown Coalition, accessed March 24, 2023, https://www.thecrownact.com/. *Natural hair* refers to hair that is not chemically processed with a relaxer, curl, or other chemical product that changes the texture of the hair. Straightened hair can still be considered natural if the straightening is achieved through heat styling because there are no chemicals involved.
15 Grayson, "Is It Fake?"; Wilson, "Beauty Rites"; Dabiri, *Twisted*.
16 Dabiri, *Twisted*.
17 Dabiri, *Twisted*.
18 Wilson, "Beauty Rites," 13.
19 *Laid* is a term that refers specifically to Black women's hair. The term applies to hair that is styled so that it lies on one's head in just the right way. It has the perfect sheen, body, and bounce.
20 Collins, *Black Feminist Thought*, 80.
21 There are professional Black women who try to embrace "nontraditional" hair colors as a way of pushing back against the arbitrary value assignment to hair color, but the association of colored hair with ratchet presentation persists.
22 *B-boy* was originally used to refer to break-dancers; breaking was a pillar of early hip-hop culture.
23 Anecdotally, referring to Black girls as overdeveloped can also become a moral judgment. I recall overhearing several conversations between grown women (including some of my relatives) who were convinced that certain girls were already having sex because, supposedly, overdevelopment was a side effect of teen girls having sex with grown men.
24 Walker, *In Search of Our Mothers' Gardens*, xi.
25 The count at the time of writing was 976,000.
26 Empressive, "The Rise of Chloe X Halle."
27 Empressive, "The Rise of Chloe X Halle."
28 This phenomenon is actually not unique to Black girl celebrities. Stars like Miley Cyrus and the Olsen twins have also been placed in this "child star gone bad" category as people struggle to reconcile their perpetual-girl image with their young adult sexual expression.
29 Halliday, "Twerk Sumn!"
30 Halliday, "Twerk Sumn!"
31 Megan Thee Stallion is known colloquially among Black women and girls as "Megan with the knees," which references her ability to twerk and "drop it" at the same time.
32 Megan Thee Stallion, "Megan Thee Stallion."
33 Halliday, "Envisioning Black Girl Futures," 72.
34 Halliday, "Envisioning Black Girl Futures," 72.

35 Kyra Gaunt's work explains the risks associated with Black girls' online sexual presentation in ways that hold social media platforms and predators accountable while avoiding demonizing Black girls. See Gaunt, "The Disclosure, Disconnect, and Digital Sexploitation of Tween Girls' Aspirational YouTube Videos."
36 Thompson, "Ten-Year-Old Designer Kheris Rogers."
37 Thompson, "Ten-Year-Old Designer Kheris Rogers."
38 Thompson, "Ten-Year-Old Designer Kheris Rogers."
39 Ford, *Liberated Threads*; Tulloch, "Style-Fashion-Dress."
40 Kari, personal interview, June 27, 2020.
41 Paige, personal interview, June 17, 2020.
42 Black girls' choreographed dance videos have been at the center of discourses of (digital) cultural appropriation. One of the most famous examples of a Black girl's work being stolen and used for others' profit is Jalaiah Harmon's "Renegade" dance. Jalaiah did finally get credit for her work after the *New York Times* published a piece highlighting her contributions to the popular/digital dance communities. See Lorenz, "The Original Renegade." Paige did not mention having any of her dances stolen, but theft and appropriation are ever-present risks for Black girls sharing their original choreography online.
43 Lorde, "Learning from the 60s," 137.

4. MAKING TIME

Part of chapter 4 draws from Wade, "Radical Curation."
1 Do you know how exciting it is for a school librarian to have a student ask for help finding books?
2 Barthold, *Black Time*; Brooks, McGee, and Schoellman, "Speculative Sankofarration."
3 CNN, "Waters Inspires Others to 'Reclaim' Their Time."
4 Ibrahim and Ahad, "Introduction," 7.
5 It's always a pejorative when non-Black people use this term.
6 This is especially the case when there is food available on a first come, first serve basis.
7 Jackson, "Sankofa Time," 105.
8 Brooks, McGee, and Schoellman, "Speculative Sankofarration," 238.
9 Brooks, McGee, and Schoellman, "Speculative Sankofarration," 242.
10 Brooks, McGee, and Schoellman, "Speculative Sankofarration," 242.
11 Prescod-Weinstein, *The Disordered Cosmos*, 57 and 60.
12 Mahadeo, "Why Is the Time Always Right for White and Wrong for Us?," 194.
13 Mahadeo, "Why Is the Time Always Right for White and Wrong for Us?," 194.
14 Morris, *Pushout*; Crenshaw, Ocean, and Nanda, "Black Girls Matter."
15 Shange, *Progressive Dystopia*.
16 This is the pseudonym assigned by the media sources and advocates bringing attention to Grace's story to maintain the anonymity of a minor.
17 Epstein, Blake, and Gonzalez, *Girlhood Interrupted*.
18 BLMIAC, Instagram Post, June 9, 2020, https://www.instagram.com/p/CBOintJlKUd/?igshid=YmMyMTA2M2Y=.

19   It is unclear who originated the #FreeGrace hashtag, as it appeared across social media platforms and was posted by multiple users.
20   Because of the pandemic, the sit-in was held outside. Despite not being able to physically occupy the inside of the courthouse, the action maintained the spirit of resistance and immovability of a more traditional sit-in.
21   "Live" is capitalized here as the name of the platform.
22   BLMIAC, Instagram Post, July 27, 2020, https://www.instagram.com/tv/CDJlO6vDPpS/?igshid=YmMyMTA2M2Y=.
23   Aimee Cox talks about this phenomenon in detail in her monograph *Shapeshifters*. This conversation has also been taken up in popular media. See also Lindsey, "Black Women Have Consistently Been Trailblazers for Social Change."
24   BLMIAC, Instagram Post, July 27, 2020.
25   I use this language based on Brennan's rationale, even though I know it is likely she used this to cover up her own bias against Grace.
26   BLMIAC, Instagram Post, July 27, 2020.
27   BLMIAC, Instagram Post, July 27, 2020.
28   BLMIAC, Instagram Post, July 27, 2020.
29   I also noticed in my own social media interactions that some people were distancing themselves from the story or refusing to advocate for Grace because of her past criminal(ized) activity.
30   BLMIAC, Instagram Post, July 27, 2020.
31   BLMIAC, Instagram Post, July 27, 2020.
32   Anderson, "Where's the Color in Kids' Lit?"
33   I first read Mildred D. Taylor's *Roll of Thunder, Hear My Cry* in third grade.
34   Balcazar, "From Prodigy Activist to Young-Adult Author."
35   Balcazar, "From Prodigy Activist to Young-Adult Author."
36   Dias, "Elle.com Has a New Boss and She's 11 Years Old."
37   Adomako, "Reimagining Black Girlhood."
38   Dias, "Elle.com Has a New Boss and She's 11 Years Old."
39   Dias, *Marley Dias Gets It Done*, 188.
40   Shange, "Black Girl Ordinary," 6; Berlant, *Cruel Optimism*, 8.
41   Shange, "Black Girl Ordinary," 6–7.
42   Blay, "How the 'Art Hoe' Movement Is Redefining the Selfie for Black Teens."
43   Sisley, "What the Hell Is an 'Art Hoe'?"
44   Frizzell, "#Arthoe."
45   Black Girl Magic, "Meet the Art Hoe Collective."
46   *Enby* is a term adopted by nonbinary people. Enby is a way of writing out the abbreviation for nonbinary (NB).
47   Chiu, "Disassembling the Gallery."
48   I recognize the tensions between "Black" and "people of color" identities, and I do not wish to conflate the two. I use the phrase *people/artists of color* when talking about the mission of the Art Hoe Collective because that is the language its founders use.
49   Wade, "Radical Curation."

50 Lara, "Of Unexplained Presences, Flying Ife Heads, Vampires, Sweat, Zombies, and Legbas," 348.
51 Nyong'o, *Afro-Fabulations*, 4.
52 Campt, *Listening to Images*, 17.
53 Lorde, "The Master's Tools Will Never Dismantle the Master's House."
54 Cooper, "The Racial Politics of Time."

CONCLUSION

1 Lorde, "Poetry Is Not a Luxury," 38.
2 *Colored people's time*, which I explain in detail in chapter 4, is a colloquial phrase that refers to Black people's willful inattention to punctuality.
3 "There are no new ideas. Only new ways of making them felt." Lorde, "Poetry Is Not a Luxury," 39.
4 Gumbs, "Sounds to Me like a Promise."

Bibliography

Adomako, Andrea. "Reimagining Black Girlhood: Literary and Digital Self-Representation." *National Political Science Review* 19, no. 2 (2018): 11–20.

Anderson, Meg. "Where's the Color in Kids' Lit? Ask the Girl with 1,000 Books (and Counting)." NPR, February 26, 2016. http://www.npr.org/sections/ed/2016/02/26/467969663/wheres-the-color-in-kids-lit-ask-the-girl-with-1-000-books-and-counting.

Asare, Janice Gassam. "Our Obsession with Black Excellence Is Harming Black People." *Forbes*, August 1, 2021. https://www.forbes.com/sites/janicegassam/2021/08/01/our-obsession-with-black-excellence-is-harming-black-people/?sh=6d0f00402fd9.

Bailey, Moya. *Misogynoir Transformed: Black Women's Digital Resistance*. New York: New York University Press, 2021.

Bailey, Moya. "#transform(ing)DH Writing and Research: An Autoethography of Digital Humanities and Feminist Ethics." *Digital Humanities Quarterly* 9, no. 2 (2015). http://www.digitalhumanities.org/dhq/vol/9/2/000209/000209.html.

Baker, Christina M., Amanda E. Staiano, and Sandra L. Calvert. "Digital Expression among Urban, Low-Income African American Adolescents." *Journal of Black Studies* 42, no. 4 (May 2011): 530–47.

Balcazar, Dahlia. "From Prodigy Activist to Young-Adult Author: Marley Dias Is Ready to Pave the Path Forward." *Bitch Media*, February 7, 2017. https://www.bitchmedia.org/article/prodigy-activist-young-adult-author/marley-dias-ready-pave-path-forward-hearken.

Banet-Weiser, Sarah. "Am I Pretty or Ugly? Girls in the Market for Self-Esteem." *Girlhood Studies* 7 (June 2014): 83–101.

Banks, Erica. "Buss It." 1501 Certified Entertainment, 2020. Accessed April 28, 2023. https://open.spotify.com/album/7B8XOfcdslOY6tcC5kcvt3.

Banks, Ingrid. *Hair Matters: Beauty, Power, and Black Women's Consciousness.* New York: New York University Press, 2000.

Barthold, Bonnie J. *Black Time: Fiction of Africa, the Caribbean, and the United States.* New Haven, CT: Yale University Press, 1981.

Benjamin, Ruha. *Race after Technology: Abolitionist Tools for the New Jim Code.* Cambridge, UK: Polity Press, 2019.

Berger, John. *Ways of Seeing.* New York: Penguin, 1972.

Berlant, Lauren. *Cruel Optimism.* Durham, NC: Duke University Press, 2011.

Black Girl Magic. "Meet the Art Hoe Collective." YouTube, 2016. https://www.youtube.com/watch?v=RHmvWR5MplM&t=11s.

Blay, Zeba. "How the 'Art Hoe' Movement Is Redefining the Selfie for Black Teens." *Huffington Post*, August 31, 2015. https://www.huffingtonpost.com/entry/art-hoe-movement-redefining-selfie_us_55df300ce4b08dc09486a020.

boyd, danah. *It's Complicated: The Social Lives of Networked Teens.* New Haven, CT: Yale University Press, 2014.

Boylorn, Robin M. "On Being at Home with Myself: Blackgirl Autoethnography as Research Praxis." *International Review of Qualitative Research* 9, no. 1 (Spring 2016): 44–58.

Bradley, Regina N. *Chronicling Stankonia: The Rise of the Hip-Hop South.* Chapel Hill: University of North Carolina Press, 2021.

Bradley, Regina N. "To Sir, with Ratchety Love: Listening to the (Dis)Respectability Politics of Rachel Jeantel." *Sounding Out!* (blog), July 1, 2013. https://soundstudiesblog.com/2013/07/01/disrespectability-politics-of-rachel-jeantel/.

Brock, Andre. *Distributed Blackness: African American Cybercultures.* New York: New York University Press, 2020.

Brooks, Kinitra, Alexis McGee, and Stephanie Schoellman. "Speculative Sankofarration: Haunting Black Women in Contemporary Horror Fiction." *Obsidian: Literature in the African Diaspora* 42, no. 1 (2016): 237–43.

Brown, Ruth Nicole. *Hear Our Truths: The Creative Potential of Black Girlhood.* Urbana: University of Illinois Press, 2013.

Brown, Ruth Nicole. "Questions Regulate/Knowledge Radiates: Black Girlhood in Saving Our Lives Hear Our Truths." *Sapphire Unbound: A Black Womanist Scholar Speaks Her Mind* (blog), June 1, 2012. http://womanistscholar.blogspot.com/2012/06/questions-regulate-knowledge-radiates.html.

Brown, Ruth Nicole, Blair Ebony Smith, Jessica L. Robinson, and Porshé R. Garner. "Doing Digital Wrongly." *American Quarterly* 70, no. 3 (2018): 395–416. https://doi.org/10.1353/aq.2018.0028.

Browne, Simone. *Dark Matters: On the Surveillance of Blackness.* Durham, NC: Duke University Press, 2015.

Butler, Tamara T. "Black Girl Cartography: Black Girlhood and Place-Making in Education Research." *Review of Research in Education* 42 (April 2018): 28–45. https://doi.org/10.3102/0091732X18762114.

Cahill, Loren S. "BlackGirl Geography." *Girlhood Studies* 12, no. 3 (December 2019): 47–62. https://doi.org/10.3167/ghs.2019.120306.

Campt, Tina. *Image Matters: Archive, Photography, and the African Diaspora in Europe*. Durham, NC: Duke University Press, 2012.

Campt, Tina. *Listening to Images*. Durham, NC: Duke University Press, 2017.

Chatelain, Marcia. *South Side Girls: Growing Up in the Great Migration*. Durham, NC: Duke University Press, 2015.

Chiu, Victoria. "Disassembling the Gallery: An Interview with the Art Hoe Collective." *The Awl*, March 11, 2016. https://medium.com/the-awl/disassembling-the-gallery-an-interview-with-the-art-hoe-collective-80e294854129.

CNN. "Waters Inspires Others to 'Reclaim' Their Time." Accessed May 19, 2023. https://www.cnn.com/videos/politics/2017/08/01/maxine-waters-reclaiming-my-time-ebof-pkg-moos.cnn.

Cobb, Jasmine Nichole. *Picture Freedom: Remaking Black Visuality in the Early Nineteenth Century*. Durham, NC: Duke University Press, 2015.

Collins, Patricia Hill. *Black Feminist Thought: Knowledge, Consciousness, and the Politics of Empowerment*. New York: Routledge, 2000.

Cooper, Brittney C. "The Racial Politics of Time." TEDWomen (video), 2016, 12:21. https://www.ted.com/talks/brittney_cooper_the_racial_politics_of_time?language=en.

Cooper, Brittney C. "(Un)Clutching My Mother's Pearls, or Ratchetness and the Residue of Respectability." In *The Crunk Feminist Collection*, edited by Brittney C. Cooper, Susana M. Morris, and Robin M. Boylorn, 217–21. New York: Feminist Press, 2017.

Cooper, Britney C., Susana M. Morris, and Robin M. Boylorn, eds. *The Crunk Feminist Collection*. New York: Feminist Press, 2017.

Cox, Aimee Meredith. *Shapeshifters: Black Girls and the Choreography of Citizenship*. Durham, NC: Duke University Press, 2015.

Craig, Maxine Leeds. *Ain't I a Beauty Queen? Black Women, Beauty, and the Politics of Race*. Oxford: Oxford University Press, 2002.

Crenshaw, Kimberlé, Priscilla Ocean, and Jyoti Nanda. *Black Girls Matter: Pushed Out, Overpoliced, and Underprotected*. New York: African American Policy Forum, 2015. https://static1.squarespace.com/static/53f20d90e4b0b80451158d8c/t/54dcc1ece4b001c03e323448/1423753708557/AAPF_BlackGirlsMatterReport.pdf.

Crowe, Nic, and Simon Bradford. "'Hanging Out in Runescape': Identity, Work and Leisure in the Virtual Playground." *Children's Geographies* 4, no. 3 (December 2006): 331–46. https://doi.org/10.1080/14733280601005740.

Cruz, Cindy. "LGBTQ Youth of Color Video Making as Radical Curriculum: A Brother Mourning His Brother and a Theory in the Flesh." *Curriculum Inquiry* 43 (2013): 441–60. https://doi.org/10.1111/curi.12022.

Dabiri, Emma. *Twisted: The Tangled History of Black Hair Culture*. New York: Harper Perennial, 2020.

Dias, Marley. "Elle.com Has a New Boss and She's 11 Years Old." *Elle*, September 19, 2016. https://www.elle.com/culture/career-politics/a38970/marley-dias-editor-letter-marley-mag/.

Dias, Marley. *Marley Dias Gets It Done: And So Can You!* New York: Scholastic, 2018.

Dill, LeConté J. "Poetic Justice: Engaging in Participatory Narrative Analysis to Find Solace in the 'Killer Corridor.'" *American Journal of Community Psychology* 55, nos. 1–2 (2014–2015): 128–35. https://doi.org/10.1007/s10464-014-9694-7.

Driscoll, Catherine. *Feminine Adolescence in Popular Culture and Cultural Theory*. New York: Columbia University Press, 2002.

Durham, Aisha. *Home with Hip Hop Feminism*. New York: Peter Lang, 2014.

Eaves, Latoya. "Black Geographic Possibilities: On a Queer Black South." *Southeastern Geographer* 57, no. 1 (Spring 2017): 80–95. https://doi.org/10.1353/sgo.2017.0007.

Elwood, Sarah. "Digital Geographies, Feminist Relationality, Black and Queer Code Studies: Thriving Otherwise." *Progress in Human Geography* 45, no. 2 (January 2020): 209–28. https://doi.org/10.1177/0309132519899733.

Empressive. "The Rise of Chloe X Halle: Chloe Bailey Cries after Being Shamed for Showing Her Body." YouTube, February 1, 2021. https://www.youtube.com/watch?v=n_jJMOSX7YI.

Epko, Ime. "17-Year-Old Who Recorded George Floyd's Murder, Darnella Frazier, Says She Is Traumatized." *The Source*, May 20, 2020. https://thesource.com/2020/05/29/darnella-frazier-traumatized/.

Epstein, Rebecca, Jamilia J. Blake, and Thalia Gonzalez. *Girlhood Interrupted: The Erasure of Black Girls' Childhood*. Washington, DC: Georgetown University Law Center, 2017. https://www.law.georgetown.edu/poverty-inequality-center/wp-content/uploads/sites/14/2017/08/girlhood-interrupted.pdf.

Everett, Anna. "Have We Become Post-racial Yet? Race and Media Technology in the Age of President Obama." In *Race after the Internet*, edited by Lisa Nakamura and Peter Chow, 146–67. New York: Routledge, 2012.

Fanon, Frantz. *Black Skin, White Masks*. London: Pluto Press, 1986.

Fleetwood, Nicole. *Troubling Vision: Performance, Visuality, and Blackness*. Chicago: University of Chicago Press, 2011.

Floridi, Luciano. "Digital Ethics Online and Off." *American Scientist* 109, no. 4 (July/August 2021): 218–22. https://doi.org/10.1511/2021.109.4.218.

Ford, Tanisha C. "Bel-Air and the Flawed Logic of 'Black Excellence.'" *Atlantic*, April 19, 2022. https://www.theatlantic.com/culture/archive/2022/04/bel-air-black-excellence-wealth/629597/.

Ford, Tanisha C. *Liberated Threads: Black Women, Style, and the Global Politics of Soul*. Chapel Hill: University of North Carolina Press, 2015.

Frizzell, Nell. "#Arthoe: The Teens Who Kickstarted a Feminist Movement." *Guardian*, August 19, 2015. https://www.theguardian.com/artanddesign/2015/aug/19/arthoe-teens-kickstart-feminist-art-movement-instagram-tumblr.

Gaunt, Kyra D. "The Disclosure, Disconnect, and Digital Sexploitation of Tween Girls' Aspirational YouTube Videos." *Journal of Black Sexuality and Relationships* 5, no. 1 (Summer 2018): 91–132. https://doi.org/10.1353/bsr.2018.0017.

Grayson, Deborah R. "Is It Fake? Black Women's Hair as Spectacle and Spec(tac)ular." *Camera Obscura: Feminism, Culture, and Media Studies* 12, no. 3 (September 1, 1995): 12–31. https://doi.org/10.1215/02705346-12-3_36-12.

Gumbs, Alexis Pauline. "Sounds to Me like a Promise: On Survival." *Brilliance Remas-*

tered (blog). Accessed March 4, 2023. https://brillianceremastered.alexispauline.com/blog/.

Halliday, Aria S., ed. *The Black Girlhood Studies Collection*. Toronto: Canadian Scholars, 2019.

Halliday, Aria S. "Envisioning Black Girl Futures: Nicki Minaj's Anaconda Feminism and New Understandings of Black Girl Sexuality in Popular Culture." *Departures in Critical Qualitative Research* 6, no. 3 (September 2017): 65–77. https://doi.org/10.1525/dcqr.2017.6.3.65.

Halliday, Aria S. "Twerk Sumn! Theorizing Black Girl Epistemology in the Body." *Cultural Studies* 34, no. 6 (January 2020): 874–91. https://doi.org/10.1080/09502386.2020.1714688.

Hernandez, Jillian. *The Aesthetics of Excess: The Art and Politics of Black and Latina Embodiment*. Durham, NC: Duke University Press, 2020.

Hill, Leah A. "Disturbing Disparities: Black Girls and the School-to-Prison Pipeline." *Fordham Law Review Online* 87, no. 11 (2018): 58–64.

Hine, Darlene Clark. "Rape and the Inner Lives of Black Women in the Middle West." *Signs* 14, no. 4 (Summer 1989): 912–20.

Ibrahim, Habiba, and Badia Ahad. "Introduction: Black Temporality in Times of Crisis." *South Atlantic Quarterly* 121, no. 1 (January 2022): 1–10.

Izadi, Elahe. "Why #BlackOutDay Took over Social Media." *Washington Post*, March 6, 2015. https://www.washingtonpost.com/news/inspired-life/wp/2015/03/06/why-blackoutday-took-over-social-media/.

Jacobs, Charlotte. "Developing the 'Oppositional Gaze': Using Critical Media Pedagogy and Black Feminist Thought to Promote Black Girls' Identity Development." *Journal of Negro Education* 85, no. 3 (July 2016): 225–38. https://doi.org/10.7709/jnegroeducation.85.3.0225.

Jackson, Antoinette T. "Sankofa Time." *Genealogy* 4, no. 4 (October 2020): 105. https://doi.org/10.3390/genealogy4040105.

Jackson, Lauren. "We Need to Talk about Digital Blackface in Reaction GIFs." *Teen Vogue*, August 2, 2017. https://www.teenvogue.com/story/digital-blackface-reaction-gifs.

Jarmon, Renina. *Black Girls Are from the Future: Essays on Race, Digital Creativity, and Pop Culture*. Washington, DC: Jarmon Media, 2013.

Johnson, Jessica Marie, and Kismet Nuñez. "Alter Egos and Infinite Literacies, Part III: How to Build a Real Gyrl in 3 Easy Steps." *Black Scholar* 45, no. 4 (2015): 47–61. https://doi.org/10.1080/00064246.2015.1080921.

Jordan-Zachery, Julia S., and Duchess Harris, eds. *Black Girl Magic beyond the Hashtag: Twenty-First-Century Acts of Self-Definition*. Tucson: University of Arizona Press, 2019.

Kearney, Mary Celeste. "Coalescing: The Development of Girls' Studies." *NWSA Journal* 21, no. 1 (Spring 2009): 1–28.

Kearney, Mary Celeste. *Girls Make Media*. New York: Routledge, 2006.

Keeling, Kara. *The Witch's Flight: The Cinematic, the Black Femme, and the Image of Common Sense*. Durham, NC: Duke University Press, 2007.

LaBennett, Oneka. *She's Mad Real: Popular Culture and West Indian Girls in Brooklyn*. New York: New York University Press, 2011.

Ladner, Joyce. *Tomorrow's Tomorrow: The Black Woman*. Garden City, NY: Doubleday, 1971.

Lara, Ana-Maurine. "Of Unexplained Presences, Flying Ife Heads, Vampires, Sweat, Zombies, and Legbas: A Meditation on Black Queer Aesthetics." *GLQ: A Journal of Lesbian and Gay Studies* 18, nos. 2–3 (2012): 347–49.

Lewis, Sheri K. "Pushing the Limits in Black Girl–Centred Research: Exploring the Methodological Possibilities of *Melt* Magazine." In *The Black Girlhood Studies Collection*, edited by Aria S. Halliday, 157–79. Toronto: Women's Press, 2019.

Lindsey, Treva B. "Black Women Have Consistently Been Trailblazers for Social Change. Why Are They So Often Relegated to the Margins?" *Time*, July 22, 2020. https://time.com/5869662/black-women-social-change/.

Lindsey, Treva B. "'One Time for My Girls': African American Girlhood, Empowerment, and Popular Visual Culture." *Journal of African American Studies* 17, no. 1 (March 2013): 22–34.

Lorde, Audre. "Learning from the 60s." In *Sister Outsider: Essays and Speeches*, 134–44. Berkeley: Crossing Press, 2007.

Lorde, Audre. "The Master's Tools Will Never Dismantle the Master's House." In *Sister Outsider: Essays and Speeches*, 110–13. Berkeley: Crossing Press, 2007.

Lorde, Audre. "Poetry Is Not a Luxury." In *Sister Outsider: Essays and Speeches*, 36–39. Berkeley: Crossing Press, 2007.

Lorenz, Taylor. "The Original Renegade." *New York Times*, February 13, 2020. https://www.nytimes.com/2020/02/13/style/the-original-renegade.html.

Love, Bettina L. "A Ratchet Lens: Black Queer Youth, Agency, Hip Hop, and the Black Ratchet Imagination." *Educational Researcher* 46, no. 9 (2017): 539–47. https://doi.org/10.3102/0013189X17736520.

Love, Bettina L. *Hip Hop's Lil' Sistas Speak: Negotiating Hip Hop Identities and Politics in the New South*. New York: Peter Lang, 2012.

Luke, Allan. "Digital Ethics Now." *Language and Literacy* 20, no. 3 (July 2018): 185–98. https://doi.org/10.20360/langandlit29416.

Mahadeo, Rahsaan. "Why Is the Time Always Right for White and Wrong for Us? How Racialized Youth Make Sense of Whiteness and Temporal Inequality." *Sociology of Race and Ethnicity* 5, no. 2 (2019): 186–99. https://doi.org/10.1177/2332649218770469.

Mazzarella, Sharon R., ed. *Girl Wide Web 2.0: Revisiting Girls, the Internet, and the Negotiation of Identity*. New York: Peter Lang, 2010.

Mazzarella, Sharon R., ed. *The Mediated Youth Reader*. New York: Peter Lang, 2016.

McKittrick, Katherine. *Dear Science and Other Stories*. Durham, NC: Duke University Press, 2021.

McKittrick, Katherine. *Demonic Grounds: Black Women and the Cartographies of Struggle*. Minneapolis: University of Minnesota Press, 2006.

McKittrick, Katherine. *Sylvia Wynter: On Being Human as Praxis*. Durham, NC: Duke University Press, 2015.

Megan Thee Stallion. "Megan Thee Stallion: Why I Speak Up for Black Women." *New York Times*, October 13, 2020. https://www.nytimes.com/2020/10/13/opinion/megan-thee-stallion-black-women.html.

Meggs, Michelle. "Is There Room for the Ratchet in the Beloved Community? If You're Not Liberating Everyone, Are You Really Talking about Freedom?" In *Womanist Ethical Rhetoric: A Call for Liberation and Social Justice in Turbulent Times*, edited by Annette D. Madlock and Cerise L. Glenn, 63–76. Lanham, MD: Lexington Books, 2021.

Mercer, Kobena. "Black Hair/Style Politics." *New Formations*, no. 3 (1987): 33–54.

Minaj, Nicki. "Hard White." Young Money/Cash Money Records, 2018. Accessed April 28, 2023. https://open.spotify.com/track/1hHbmfNfXIwHyHCYO8ae3I.

Morgan, Jennifer L. "Archives and Histories of Racial Capitalism: An Afterword." *Social Text* 33, no. 4 (2015): 153–61. https://doi.org/10.1215/01642472-3315862.

Morris, Edward. "'Ladies' or 'Loudies': Perceptions and Experiences of Black Girls in Classrooms." *Youth and Society* 38, no. 4 (June 2007): 490–515.

Morris, Monique. *Pushout: The Criminalization of Black Girls in Schools*. New York: New Press, 2016.

Nelly. "Hot in Herre." Universal Records, 2002. Accessed April 28, 2023. https://open.spotify.com/track/04KTF78FFg8sOHC1BADqbY.

New You Brands. "Girls from around the World Participated in Live Conversation Featuring First Lady Michelle Obama." YouTube, October 11, 2016. https://www.youtube.com/watch?v=iY4-8yS59r0.

Noble, Safiya. *Algorithms of Oppression: How Search Engines Reinforce Racism*. New York: New York University Press, 2018.

Nyong'o, Tavia. *Afro-Fabulations: The Queer Drama of Black Life*. New York: New York University Press, 2019.

O'Grady, Lorraine. "Olympia's Maid: Reclaiming Black Female Subjectivity." *Afterimage* 20 (1992): 14–23.

Owens, Tammy C., Durell M. Callier, Jessica L. Robinson, and Porshé R. Garner. "Towards an Interdisciplinary Field of Black Girlhood Studies." *Departures in Critical Qualitative Research* 6, no. 3 (September 1, 2017): 116–32. https://doi.org/10.1525/dcqr.2017.6.3.116.

Prescod-Weinstein, Chanda. *The Disordered Cosmos: A Journey into Dark Matter, Spacetime, and Dreams Deferred*. New York: Bold Type Books, 2021.

Pritchard, Eric Darnell. *Fashioning Lives: Black Queers and the Politics of Literacy*. Carbondale: Southern Illinois University Press, 2017.

Projansky, Sarah. *Spectacular Girls: Media Fascination and Celebrity Culture*. New York: New York University Press, 2014.

Rockett, Ali, and Reed Williams. "Wave of Violence Continues in Richmond with 22 People Slain in the Past Two Months." *Richmond Times-Dispatch*, October 4, 2020. https://richmond.com/news/local/crime-and-courts/wave-of-violence-continues-in-richmond-with-22-people-slain-in-the-past-two-months/article_54ec5e1c-a586-5d4b-bea7-4020a8fd6a07.html.

Rooks, Noliwe M. *Hair Raising: Beauty, Culture, and African American Women*. New Brunswick, NJ: Rutgers University Press, 1996.

Ruckenstein, Minna. "Spatial Extensions of Childhood: From Toy Worlds to Online Communities." *Children's Geographies* 11, no. 4 (June 2013): 476–89. https://doi.org/10.1080/14733285.2013.812309.

Ruffin, Ravon. "Digital Archives: Radical Acts of Self Preservation." Paper Presented at the Maryland Institute for Technology in the Humanities' Digital Dialogues, University of Maryland, College Park, October 25, 2016. https://vimeo.com/188888033.

Saar, Malika Saada, Rebecca Epstein, Lindsay Rosenthal, and Yasmin Vafa. *The Sexual Abuse to Prison Pipeline: The Girls' Story*. Washington, DC: Georgetown University Law Center,

2015. https://forwomen.org/wp-content/uploads/2015/05/documents_Sexual-Abuse-to-Prison-Pipeline-The-Girls-Story-2015.pdf.

Senft, Theresa M., and Nancy K. Baym. "What Does the Selfie Say? Investigating a Global Phenomenon." *International Journal of Communication* 9 (January 2015): 1588–1601.

Shange, Savannah. "Black Girl Ordinary." *Transforming Anthropology* 27, no. 1 (March 2019): 3–21. https://doi.org/10.1111/traa.12143.

Shange, Savannah. *Progressive Dystopia: Abolition, Antiblackness, and Schooling in San Francisco*. Durham, NC: Duke University Press, 2019.

Simmons, LaKisha. *Crescent City Girls: The Lives of Young Black Women in Segregated New Orleans*. Chapel Hill: University of North Carolina Press, 2015.

Sisley, Dominique. "What the Hell Is an 'Art Hoe'?" *Dazed*, August 18, 2015. http://www.dazeddigital.com/artsandculture/article/25862/1/the-new-art-movement-empowering-poc.

Smith, Ashley L. "Theorizing Black Girlhood." In *The Black Girlhood Studies Collection*, edited by Aria S. Halliday, 21–44. Toronto: Women's Press, 2019.

Squires, Catherine R. "Rethinking the Black Public Sphere: An Alternative Vocabulary for Multiple Public Spheres." *Communication Theory* 12, no. 4 (November 2002): 446–68.

Stallings, L. H. "Hip Hop and the Black Ratchet Imagination." *Palimpsest: A Journal on Women, Gender, and the Black International* 2, no. 2 (2013): 135–39. https://doi.org/10.1353/pal.2013.0026.

Steele, Catherine Knight. "Black Bloggers and Their Varied Publics: The Everyday Politics of Black Discourse Online." *Television and New Media* 19, no. 2 (February 2018): 112–27. https://doi.org/10.1177/1527476417709535.

Steele, Catherine Knight. "The Digital Barbershop: Blogs and Online Oral Culture within the African American Community." *Social Media + Society* 2, no. 4 (October 2016). https://doi.org/10.1177/2056305116683205.

Stokes, Carla. "Representin' in Cyberspace: Sexual Scripts, Self-Definition, and Hip-Hop Culture in Black American Adolescent Girls' Home Pages." *Culture, Health, and Sexuality* 9 (February 2007): 169–84.

"#TheBlackout—Home of Blackout Day." Tumblr, March 6, 2017. https://tumblr.theblackout.org/post/114966275331/official-blackoutday-masterpost-created-march.

Thiel-Stern, Shayla. *From the Dance Hall to Facebook: Teen Girls, Mass Media, and Moral Panic in the United Sates, 1905–2010*. Amherst: University of Massachusetts Press, 2014.

Thomas, Greg. "PROUD FLESH Inter/Views: Sylvia Wynter." PROUDFLESH: *A New Afrikan Journal of Culture, Politics, and Consciousness*, no. 4 (2006). https://www.africaknowledgeproject.org/index.php/proudflesh/article/view/202.

Thompson, Giania. "Ten-Year-Old Designer Kheris Rogers on Why She's Flexin' in My Complexion." *The Undefeated*, August 7, 2017. https://theundefeated.com/features/ten-year-old-designer-kheris-rogers-flexin-in-my-complexion/.

Thompson, Krista. *Shine: The Visual Economy of Light in African Diasporic Aesthetic Practice*. Durham, NC: Duke University Press, 2015.

Tolliver, S. R. "Breaking Binaries: #BlackGirlMagic and the Black Ratchet Imagination." *Journal of Language and Literacy Education* 15, no. 1 (Spring 2019): 1–26.

Trouillot, Michel-Rolph. *Silencing the Past: Power and the Production of History*. Boston: Beacon Press, 1995.

Tulloch, Carol. "Style-Fashion-Dress: From Black to Post-Black." *Fashion Theory* 14, no. 3 (2010): 273–303. https://doi.org/10.2752/175174110X12712411520179.

Underwood, Stephen. "Is Black Excellence Killing Us?" *Essence*, October 23, 2020. https://www.essence.com/op-ed/is-black-excellence-killing-us/.

Wade, Ashleigh Greene. "Indigo Child Runnin' Wild: Willow Smith's Archive of Black Girl Magic." *National Political Science Review* 19, no. 2 (2018): 21–33.

Wade, Ashleigh Greene. "Not New to This: A Genealogical Approach to Black Girls' Media Production." *Camera Obscura: Feminism, Culture, and Media Studies* 37, no. 1 (2022): 1–29.

Wade, Ashleigh Greene. "Radical Curation: Making Space for Black Childhood(s) in the Art Hoe Collective." *Visual Arts Research* 47, no. 1 (2021): 13–28.

Walker, Alice. *In Search of Our Mothers' Gardens: Womanist Prose*. New York: Harcourt Brace Jovanovich, 1983.

Wallis, Brian, and Deborah Willis. *African American Vernacular Photography: Selections from the Daniel Cowin Collection*. New York: International Center for Photography, 2006.

Weisbard, Eric. "Kyra Gaunt, on Played: Twerking w/ Aria Halliday, Regina Bradley, and Alisha Jones for PMBiP 11/17." YouTube, 2020. https://www.youtube.com/watch?v=J33Zvac8P-I.

Williams, Heather Andrea. *Self-Taught: African American Education in Slavery*. Chapel Hill: University of North Carolina Press, 2005.

Williams, Raymond. "Structures of Feeling." In *Marxism and Literature*, 128–35. Oxford: Oxford University Press, 1977.

Wilson, Judith. "Beauty Rites: Towards an Anatomy of Culture in African American Women's Art." *International Review of African American Art* 11, no. 3 (1994): 11–26.

Wynter, Sylvia. "Ethno or Socio Poetics." *Alcheringa* 2, no. 2 (1976): 78–94.

Index

activism, 17, 107–8, 115, 118–19, 122–24, 131
Adams, Sage, 120
advocacy, 106
affect, 11, 15, 25–26, 77–79, 90, 101
African American Policy Forum, 136n9
African American Vernacular English (AAVE), 85, 120, 135n52
Afrofuturism, 109
agency, 55–60, 82, 93–100, 107–8, 132
algorithms, 4–5, 20, 23. *See also* social media
alienation, 57–58
anaconda feminism, 98–99
anonymity, 4, 24, 140n28. *See also* privacy; pseudonyms
archives: and the everyday, 82–83; informal construction of, 63–66; professionalization of, 64–65; and public exhibition, 80–82; and temporality, 82–83; and urgency, 66, 128–29
Art Hoe Collective, 17, 107, 120–23, 144n48
artistry, 10, 17. *See also* creativity
Auntie Maxine. *See* Waters, Maxine
authenticity, 57, 80–82

Autopoiesis and Cognition (Maturana and Varela), 10
Awl, The, 121

Bailey, Chloe, 94–95
Bailey, Halle, 94
Bailey, Moya, 7, 134n10
Banks, Erica, 94
Barthold, Bonnie J., 109
Basketball Wives, 87–88
Baym, Nancy, 70
B-boy/B-girl stance, 92, plate 15
beauty standards, 69, 84–85, 89–90. *See also* body image
Becton, Dejerria, 137n10
Beyoncé, 92, 94
Bibles, 64–65, 76, 140n14
"Black Beatles" (Rae Sremmurd), 54
Black feminism, 12–13, 20, 32–33, 58. *See also* feminism
Black girl autopoetics (BGA): and archival processes, 129; and art, 131–32; and Black feminism, 12–13; and community, 70;

Black girl autopoetics (*continued*)
creative force of, 9–11, 63–64, 72, 92, 103–4, 122, 132; and digital ethics, 26; and reinvention, 59–60, 73–74, 100, 107, 119; and self-making, 87; and space-making, 15, 31–33; and temporality, 14–15, 107–8, 114–15; and vernacular image-making, 63–64. *See also* poetics

#BlackGirlMagic, 12, 119, 135n39

Black girl ordinary, 119

Black girls: and ethical standards, 20; and masculinity, 140n35; mentorship for, 31; perceptions of, 4, 36–37, 77, 85, 113; potential futures, 123–24; and precarity, 33, 63, 113–15; and sexuality, 5–6, 67–68, 74; and temporality, 17. *See also* childhood; early adultification; girlhood

"Black is beautiful," 69

Black joy, 77–80

"Black Lady" trope, 91

Black Lives Matter in All Capacities (BLMIAC), 17, 107, 111–17

"Black Lives Matter" slogan, 44–45

Blackness, 6–8, 31, 107, 109–10, 129

#BlackoutDay, 68–70

Black Power movement, 69, 90

Black Time (Barthold), 109

Blay, Yaba, 48

bodily autonomy, 38–42, 49, 57–58

body image, 86, 95. *See also* beauty standards

bonchinche, 26

Bookmarks, 124

boyd, danah, 56

braggadocio, 101

branding, 51–52, 85, 102–3

Brennan, Mary Ellen, 111, 114

Brooks, Kinitra, 109–10

Brown, Ruth Nicole, 12–13

"Buss It" challenge, 94, 96

Butler, Tamara T., 32

BuzzFeed, 47

Caesar, Shirley, 1–2

cameras, access to, 66, 82. *See also* smartphones

Campt, Tina, 67, 123

captions, 69, 71–72, 75

Cardi B, 79

cartographies, 32–33, 59–60, 127. *See also* multilayered geographies; physical-digital-conceptual connection

catcalling, 48

cell phone bans, 35–36, 42–43

challenges, 54, 71, 76, 94, 141n40. *See also* social media; *specific challenges*

childhood: legal boundaries of, 6–7; reclamation of, 103, 114–15, 125, 132; reminders of, 71; and rites of passage, 74. *See also* Black girls; early adultification; girlhood

"child star gone bad" trope, 142n28

civil rights movement, 90

Clinton, Hillary, 118

college reveal videos, 76–77

Collins, Patricia Hill, 91

colorism, 69–70, 100. *See also* racism

conceptual conditioning, 52

Cooper, Brittney, 89, 125

Copeland, Misty, 118

Cosby Show, 95

COVID-19, 35, 73, 75, 93–94, 99, 111–12, 144n20, plate 3

Cox, Aimee, 144n23

CP (colored people's) time, 108–9, 130. *See also* temporality

creativity, 5–6, 10–11, 14–16, 63–64, 103–4, 132. *See also* artistry

crime: depictions of, 66; evidence of criminality, 114–15; geographic distribution of, 35

criminalization, 5, 23, 111–12

CROWN Act, 89, 142n14

Cruz, Cindy, 80

cultural appropriation, 47–48

cultural dissemblance, 56

Cyrus, Miley, 142n28

dancing, 79, 95–96, 102, 143n42. *See also* twerking

death, images of, 44–45, 133n6

detention centers, 114. *See also* school-to-prison pipeline

Dias, Marley, 17, 116–19, 124

digital blackface, 23

digital dissemblance, 55–56

digital garreting, 55–59
digital-physical divisions, 16, 34, 60, 139n50
digital spaces: conceptual mapping of, 44–45; dismissive attitude toward, 85; and embodiment, 33–34; overlaps with physical space, 34, 46–48, 53, 57–58; possibilities of, 54, 127; protection of, 43–44, 58; replication of offline oppression, 32; and sexuality, 46. *See also* social media; technology
digital utopianism, 33–34
Dill, LeConté, 7
disabilities, 111–12
discipline, 22, 35–40, 42–43. *See also* dress codes; surveillance
DJ Suede the Remix God, 1–2
#DontRushChallenge, 76–77
double-consciousness, 10
dreams, 75–76
dress codes, 38–40, 97. *See also* discipline; schools
Du Bois, W. E. B., 10, 81
Durham, Aisha, 11
DuVernay, Ava, 118

early adultification, 4, 20–21, 71, 73, 93, 96, 113–14, 123–24. *See also* Black girls; childhood
education: academic achievements, 74–75, plate 7; access to, 74; and childhood, 6–9; and disability, 111; policing of, 111; restructuring curriculum, 118. *See also* graduation; scholarships; schools
elections, 53–54
Elle, 117–18, 124
Empowering Black Girls (EBG) summer camp, 51
ephemerality, 56, 65, 88, 138n43
ethics, 15–16, 19–27, 138n23. *See also* institutional review boards (IRBs); power differentials; research collaborators
ethnographic self-reflexivity, 20
ethnopoetics, 9

Facebook, 3, 56, 134n8
facial recognition, 23
Fanon, Frantz, 10
"fast Black girl" trope, 96

fatphobia, 86
femininity, 38, 73, 92, 140n35. *See also* gender; masculinity
feminism, 12–13, 47, 86, 98. *See also* Black feminism
Finstas, 56–57. *See also* Instagram
flexin, 100–103
Flexin' in My Complexion, 100
Flo Milli, 79
Floyd, George, 2–4, 133n3, 133n6
"Formation" (Beyoncé), 92
Frazier, Darnella, 2–5, 133n3, 133n6, 134n11
#FreeGrace, 107, 111–16, 144n19

garreting, 55–59
Gaunt, Kyra, 6, 143n35
gaze, 15, 20, 25–26, 90, 120
gender: expression, 6–7; policing of, 38, 92; signifiers of, 9. *See also* femininity
gender-bending, 92
gentrification, 35, 128. *See also* socioeconomic status
"Get Ready with Me" genre, 78–79
"Get Up 10" (Cardi B), 79
girlhood: distinctions from womanhood, 12, 20–21, 87–88, 135n42; perceptions of, 94; and sexual agency, 97; theories of, 67, 135n42. *See also* Black girls; childhood
Google AdSense, 6
graduation, 72, 74–77, plates 6–10. *See also* education; schools
Green, T'Von, 68
Green Book, 128
#GRWM. *See* "Get Ready with Me" genre
Gumbs, Alexis Pauline, 132

hairstyles, 62, 69, 89–90, 140n25, 140n29, 142n19, 142n21. *See also* kinky hair; natural hair
Halliday, Aria, 98
Hampton University, 36
"Hard White" (Minaj), 98
Harmon, Jalaiah, 143n42
Harris, Duchess, 12
hashtag appropriation, 121
hashtags, 68, 70, 121

haters, 80
Henson, Taraji P., 100
heteropatriarchy, 3, 9–10, 15, 107, 138n27
Hine, Darlene Clark, 56
hip-hop, 1–2, 92
"Hold My Mule" (Caesar), 1–2
"Hot Girl Summer," 98, plates 18–19
"Hot in Herre" (Nelly), 94
hyper(in)visibility: intensification of, 93; paradoxes of, 7, 85–87, 104–5, 130; and public/private binaries, 23; as resistance, 16, 86–87, 89, 130; risks of, 5, 55–56, 59; and sexuality, 93–100. *See also* misogynoir

"I Bet You Won't" (Level), 79
identity, 4, 14, 23, 27, 39, 67–68, 86, 94, 104, 120, 128, 130
influencers, 101–2
Instagram: and activism, 112; affordances of, 8, 67, 85–86, 138n44, 141n3; as archive, 56, 94, 102, 120–21, 129; and circulation of images, 68; social norms of, 8–9, 75. *See also* Finstas
Instagram Live, 112–13
institutional review boards (IRBs), 19–20, 24, 26–27, 135n2. *See also* ethics
internalized misogyny, 46
International Women's Day, 44

Jacobs, Harriet, 55–59
Jarmon, Renina, 58
Jennings, John, 110
Jordan-Zachery, Julia, 12

Kearney, Mary Celeste, 14
Keeling, Kara, 139n4
Keys, Alicia, 100
kinky hair, 62–63, 69–70, 139n4, 140n25, 140n29. *See also* hairstyles

laptop access programs, 50
laughter, 71, 80
Liberty Prep: curriculum at, 32, 136n7; demographics of, 51, 136n3; and discipline, 21–22, 35–41, 49–50; student community at, 62; volunteers at, 137n20

Lil' Kim, 97, plate 16
literacy, 105–7
lit expression, 77–80
Lorde, Audre, 104, 127
Love & Hip Hop, 87–88

Mahadeo, Rahsaan, 110
Mannequin Challenge, 54
Manuel, ShaMichael, 5
Marley Dias Gets It Done (Dias), 118
Marley Mag, 117–18
masculinity, 74, 140n35. *See also* femininity
Mazarella, Sharon, 14
McGee, Alexis, 109
McKittrick, Katherine, 10, 55, 57
media erasure, 63, 68, 77, 80–81, 116–17
media literacy, 22, 36–37, 62
media representation, 62, 68, 129, 137n13, 139n4. *See also* representation
Megan Thee Stallion, 98, 142n31, plates 18–19
Meggs, Michelle, 89
memes, 4, 31, 115
memory, 1, 14–15, 21, 77, 82, 93, 105, 128
Mende, 90
Minaj, Nicki, 98–99, plate 20
misogynoir: definitions of, 134n10; and dress code, 38–39; impacts on health, 11, 131–32; and paradoxes, 4, 86–87; resistance to, 55, 57, 77, 130; and school rules, 41; and sexuality, 73, 85. *See also* hyper(in)visibility; racism; white supremacy
Mnuchin, Steven, 108
Morgan, Jennifer, 82
MTV, 78
multilayered geographies, 32–34, 59–60. *See also* cartographies
My Brother's Keeper initiative, 113
My Super Sweet 16, 78

National Signing Day campaign, 76
natural hair, 69–70. *See also* hairstyles
Naturally Golden, 79
Nelly, 94
Netflix, 124
New Orleans, 33
New Republic (Wiley), 7

New York Times, 98, 143n42
Nkiru, Jenn, 121–22
Noble, Safiya, 5
nonbinary people, 74, 120, 144n46
Now This, 3
Nyong'o, Lupita, 68, 100

Obama, Barack, 113
Obama, Michelle, 44, 76, 91, 141n39
objectification, 93, 98. *See also* self-objectification; sexualization
O'Grady, Lorraine, 62–63
Oleita, Eva, 17, 111–12, 114–15, 123
Olsen twins, 142n28
#1000BlackGirlBooks, 17, 107, 116–19, 123
oral traditions, 26–27, 82. *See also* storytelling

Parkwood Entertainment, 94
patriarchy, 3, 9–10, 15, 107, 138n27
physical-digital-conceptual connection, 48, 52, 128. *See also* cartographies
play, 15, 102, 131–32
poetics, 8–10. *See also* Black girl autopoetics (BGA)
"Poetry Is Not a Luxury" (Lorde), 127
police violence, 2–3, 45, 112, 115, 133n4, 137n10. *See also* violence
Pollard, Taylor, 100
pornography, 6
Posing Beauty (Willis), 7
poverty, 35, 41, 135n5. *See also* socioeconomic status
power differentials, 20–22, 40–42. *See also* ethics
precarity, 75, 115
Prescod-Weinstein, Chanda, 110
pride, 41, 68, 100–103
privacy, 14, 20, 23–25, 35, 136n10. *See also* anonymity
"Professional Black Girl" (Blay), 48
professionalism, 38, 91
prom, 46, 72–74, plates 2–5
pseudonyms, 21–22, 139. *See also* anonymity
PTSD, 114
Pulliam, Keshia Knight, 95–96
punctuality, 109. *See also* temporality

#quarantinebae, 99
queerness, 86, 120–22

racism: familiarity of, 11, 31, 47; internalization of, 68; perceptions of, 47; and photographic imagery, 66–67. *See also* colorism; misogynoir; stereotypes; white supremacy
Rae Sremmurd, 54
rap music, 79, 98
ratchet feminism, 89
ratchet performativity, 87–92, 130, plates 12–14
ratchet womanism, 89
reality television, 87
real-name policies, 3–4, 134n8. *See also* usernames
refusal, 87, 89–90, 101, 104
representation, 13, 25–26, 62, 66, 68–70, 117–18, 123, 129–30, 137n13, 139n4
research collaborators, 21, 136n6. *See also* ethics
respectability, 88, 104
Reynolds, Judeah, 2–3, 133n3
Rhimes, Shonda, 68
Richmond: and Black cultural production, 7–8; connections to, 32; socioeconomic divides in, 49–50, 137n16
Rogers, Kheris, 100, 103
Russell, Ama, 17, 111–12, 114–15, 123

sankofa, 109–10
sass, 91–92, plate 13
#SayHerName, 112
Schoellman, Stephanie, 109
scholarships, 50–52. *See also* education
schools: central role of, 84; classroom sizes, 35–36; curricular development, 22; and discipline, 35–38, 40, 63; employees of, 29–31, 36–37; honor codes, 49; racial makeup of, 55; resources at, 111; safety in, 41–42. *See also* dress codes; education; graduation
school-to-prison pipeline, 63, 74, 123–24. *See also* detention centers
self-curation, 80–82, 85–86
self-definition, 129–30
selfies, 53, 67–71, 73–74, 85–86
self-objectification, 98–99. *See also* objectification

self-reflexivity, 20, 23
Senft, Theresa, 70
Seventeen, 62–63
sexuality, 46, 74, 93–100, 130
sexualization, 5–6, 93, 99. *See also* objectification
sexual violence, 45, 99, 138n27
Shange, Savannah, 119
Simmons, LaKisha, 33–34
slavery, disruption of, 65, 108, 130
slutshaming, 94–95
smartphones, 65–66, 140n19. *See also* cameras, access to
Snapchat: affordances of, 52–53, 67; audiences of, 56; and ephemerality, 56, 65, 88, 138n43; group content creation, 71; launch of, 8, 31, 62; social norms of, 46, 61
social media: and activism, 115, 124–25; as archive, 56, 65, 82; as branding tool, 102–3; corporations, 13–14; and curation, 16, 56–57; and future opportunity, 51–52; privacy settings, 23–24; as storytelling, 63–64; and surveillance, 52; training for use, 51–52, 84–85. *See also* algorithms; challenges; digital spaces; usernames; *specific platforms*
socioeconomic status, 20, 49, 91. *See also* gentrification; poverty
space-making, 31–32, 60, 128
Spring Valley High School, 137n10
Squires, Catherine R., 57
Steele, Catherine Knight, 57
stereotypes, 6, 53, 88. *See also* racism
storytelling, 61–64, 66, 82. *See also* oral traditions
Stunna Girl, 79
surveillance, 42–43, 50, 52, 57. *See also* discipline

Taylor, Breonna, 112, 115
technology: access to, 50, 60, 66–67; as mundane, 1–2, 12; and play, 15; and representation, 137n13. *See also* digital spaces
technophobia, 56
temporality: and agency, 109–10, 112–13, 115–17,

122; as cyclical, 118; disruptions of, 108–9, 116, 130; reclamation of, 130; wasted time, 105–6
texturism, 69–70. *See also* colorism
Thomas, Greg, 9
Thompson, Sharkeisha, 5
TikTok, 76, 94
tokenization, 62–63
trap music, 79
trauma, 3–4
trauma porn, 62–63, 139n5
Triller, 1, 14, 133n1
Trump, Donald, 53–54, 108, 138n36
Truth, Sojurner, 81
Tumblr, 68, 120–21
twerking, 5–6, 94, 98. *See also* dancing
Twitter, 4, 116

Union, Gabrielle, 91
United States: demographics of, 7–8, 134n21; heteropatriarchal society in, 97; image economy of, 62–63; restrictions on space, 33; sociopolitical climate of 2020, 75
unmirroring, 62–63
usernames, 3–4, 21, 24, 43. *See also* real-name policies; social media
ussies, 71. *See also* selfies

Valentín, Al, 26
vernacular image-making, 16, 63–68, 80–82, 128
violence, 2–3, 30, 44. *See also* police violence
Virginia Commonwealth University, 7
Virginia Museum of Fine Arts, 7
visuality, 13
vlogging, 78

walkability, 49
Walker, Alice, 93
Walker, Madame C. J., 89, 142n14
Wallis, Brian, 66
Waters, Maxine, 108, 110
West Academy, 32, 49–53
Whisper Challenge, 71, plate 1
white clothing, 75, 141n38

whiteness, 85, 90
white supremacy, 3, 11, 73, 88–89, 107, 117, 123, 130. *See also* misogynoir; racism
Wiley, Kehinde, 7
Willis, Deborah, 7, 66
Wilmore, Larry, 118
womanism, 93
Women's History Month, 103
world-making, 11, 14

World Star Hip Hop, 5
Wynter, Sylvia, 9–10

Yoruba, 90
"You Name It" meme, 1–2
YouTube: as archives, 65, 129; content policies, 6; group content creation, 71; makeup and hair tutorials, 101; privacy settings, 9, 136n10; and vlogging, 78